EXTRAORDINARY BLACK AMERICANS

FROM COLONIAL TO CONTEMPORARY TIMES

BY SUSAN ALTMAN

Consultants

Tony Martin, Ph.D.,
Professor and Chairman of
Department of Black Studies,
Wellesley College,
Wellesley, Massachusetts

Lynell Hemphill, M.A.,
Education, Literary Consultant,
Chicago, Illinois

 CHILDRENS PRESS ®

CHICAGO

Dedication

This book is dedicated to my parents, Sophie and Norman Altman, who tried to instill in their children a sense of justice, an appreciation of freedom, and a respect for the rights of others.

It is further dedicated to the memory of Addie Mae Collins, Denise McNair, Carole Robertson, Cynthia Wesley, Emmett Till, and Godfrey Sicelo Dlomo, six young people whom freedom failed to reach and justice failed to protect.

Project Editor: Alice Osinski
Copy Editors: E. Russell Primm,
             Ann Heinrichs
Indexer: Ann Heinrichs
Designer: Lindaanne Donohoe
Typesetter: Graphic Connections, Inc.
Engraver: Rayson Films Inc.

Library of Congress Cataloging-in-Publication Data

Altman, Susan R.
  Extraordinary Black Americans from Colonial to Contemporary Times / by Susan R. Altman.
      p.   cm.
  Includes index.
  Summary: Presents short biographies of black Americans from colonial to contemporary times, highlighting their personal achievements and contributions to the growth of American society.
  ISBN 0-516-00581-2
  1. Afro-Americans—Biography—Juvenile literature. [1. Afro-Americans—Biography.] I. Title.
E185.96.A56   1989   89-11977
[B]   CIP
[920]   AC

Contents

Foreword

Slavery was instituted in the United States for the purpose of providing free labor for the building of the nation. Although the lives of black slaves were rooted in the plantations, slaves managed to create a life apart from their masters. Not content merely to survive, they refused to allow others to control their thoughts and feelings. They resisted slavery—not only through violence and by running away but also in their hearts.

The desire for freedom, which drove slaves and "free" blacks to fight for their rights, carried over into their lives after slavery was outlawed and still continues today. The eighty-five biographies in this book reveal the lives of such people as Harriet Tubman and Nat Turner, who resisted enslavement, and Mary McLeod Bethune and Martin Luther King, Jr., who struggled to create a better life for all people.

As you read the following biographies, you will learn how black women and men tried to advance in society by using every strategy available to the normal, intelligent mind. You will understand why the failure of blacks to enjoy equal opportunity in America was not the result of a lack of ability.

This book provides a record of the women and men who struggled against the odds—a record of the determination that enabled them to turn high purpose into high achievement in an impressive number of fields.

Despite the lingering effects of slavery, black people—and all lovers of freedom—can take inspiration from Susan Altman's *Extraordinary Black Americans from Colonial to Contemporary Times.*

Sterling Stuckey
Senior Fellow
Smithsonian Institution
Washington, D.C.
Fall 1988

Preface

America is home to people of almost every race, religion, and nationality. Some, like the Indians and the Eskimos, have been here for thousands of years. Others, who arrived later, came in the hope of finding riches, adventure, and a new life. And some, fleeing war, famine, and persecution, sought only safety and a chance to survive. Black people alone were brought here unwillingly, stolen from their homes and forced to live as slaves.

Yet, in spite of this cruel beginning, black Americans have played a major role in defining and shaping American beliefs, traditions, and customs. From the beginning they have helped insure the nation's security and economic well-being. They are among our earliest explorers and have been among the first people to expand and settle the frontier.

Of the people profiled in these pages, many were selected because of the contributions they made to our life and culture. Others were chosen because of the part they played at critical points in our history. And some are presented because they allowed the author to better explore the black presence in areas where often it has been ignored.

This book represents but a small fraction of the thousands of black Americans who have added to the growth and development of this country. Of those not mentioned, some are well known, and their lives and work have been dealt with extensively elsewhere. Many more remain anonymous. In some cases the record of their accomplishments has been left to fade under the glare of onrushing events. In other cases, no record existed in the first place.

Many of the men and women this book describes overcame incredible hardships with little to sustain them but their own courage and determination. How many others tried but were crushed under the wheels of unremitting repression will never be known. But some did survive. Some did triumph.

Like other racial, religious, and ethnic groups, black Americans have made their presence felt in fields ranging from science and industry to literature, education, religion, and the arts. Yet, it may be that the main contribution of black Americans has not been in any specific area but rather to democracy itself. For in the struggle to secure, protect, and defend their own rights, black Americans have helped guarantee the rights of everyone else.

Susan Altman
Washington, D.C.

List of Abbreviations

AME	African Methodist Episcopal Church
CORE	Congress of Racial Equality
DAR	Daughters of the American Revolution
MFDP	Mississippi Freedom Democratic Party
MIA	Montgomery Improvement Association
NAACP	National Association for the Advancement of Colored People
NACW	National Association of Colored Women
NASA	National Aeronautics and Space Administration
NORAD	North American Air Defense Command
NYA	National Youth Administration
OAAU	Organization of Afro-American Unity
OCS	Officers' Candidate School
PUSH	People United to Serve Humanity
SCLC	Southern Christian Leadership Conference
SNCC	Student Nonviolent Coordinating Committee
UCLA	University of California in Los Angeles
UN	United Nations
UNIA	Universal Negro Improvement and Conservation Association

Estevanico

Explorer
?-1539

Panfilo de Narváez left Spain in 1528 with 600 men. When his expedition finally reached the area of North America that is now Florida, there were only 400 left; and by the time it arrived in what is now Texas, their number had been cut to eighty. A year later, only four men were still alive—among them, an African slave named Estevanico, or Little Steven.

Born in Azemmour, Morocco, Estevanico had been captured and taken to Spain when he was about thirteen years old. His master, Andrés Dorantes, was a Spanish explorer and adventurer who took Estevanico with him when he joined Narváez's expedition to the New World.

Narváez and his men were looking for gold and jewels. What they found, instead, was starvation, disease, and death. For the next eight years, Estevanico and three other survivors wandered throughout the Southwest, across what is now Texas and Mexico to the Gulf of California. About 1536 they reached a Spanish settlement in Culiacán, Mexico. From there, they went to Mexico City, where they met Don Antonio de Mendoza, the Spanish viceroy. He listened to the Indian stories about the Seven Cities of Cibola supposedly made of gold.

Fascinated by the stories, Mendoza sent out an expedition under Father Marcos de Niza. Estevanico traveled ahead of the main group and, using Indian runners, sent back crosses indicating how near he was to the Seven Cities. The closer he got, the larger the crosses he sent back. Then, suddenly, all communication from him stopped. Later, two wounded Indians returned and said that Estevanico had died in an Indian attack.

Exactly what happened, no one knows. One thing is certain: it was Estevanico who guided the first expedition through the American Southwest, and it was his tales of the legendary Seven Cities of Cibola that encouraged others to explore what later became the states of Texas, New Mexico, Arizona, Colorado, Oklahoma, and Kansas.

Lucy Terry Prince

Poet
1733-1821

The Bar's Fight

August 'twas the twenty-fifth
Seventeen hundred forty-six
The Indians did in ambush lay
Some very valient men to slay
Twas nigh unto Sam Dickinson's mill,
The Indians there five men did kill
The names of whom I'll not leave out
Samuel Allen like a hero fout
And though he was so brave and bold
His face no more shall we behold
Eleazer Hawks was killed outright
Before he had time to fight
Before he did the Indians see

Was shot and killed immediately
Oliver Amsden he was slain

Which caused his friends much grief
    and pain
Simeon Amsden they found dead
Not many rods off from his head.
Adonijah Gillet, we do hear
Did lose his life which was so dear
John Saddler fled across the water
And so escaped the dreadful slaughter
Eunice Allen see the Indians coming
And hoped to save herself by running
And had not her petticoats stopt her
The awful creatures had not cotched her,
And tommyhawked her on the head
And left her on the ground for dead.
Young Samuel Allen, Oh! lack-a-day
Was taken and carried to Canada [1]

T his poem describes an Indian attack on Deerfield, Massachusetts, a small settlement on the western border of the Massachusetts Colony. Written by Lucy Terry, a sixteen-year-old slave girl, the poem is considered to be the best description of the account on record.

The attack occurred in 1746 during the French and Indian War. Although Lucy Terry's poem describing the massacre was not published until 1855, it was a favorite in colonial New England. Often, it was read at town meetings and on various social occasions to keep alive the memory of the historic attack.

The events Lucy Terry described in her poem were not too far from some of those in her own life. She had been kidnapped from her home in Africa when she was only five and sold to a family in Deerfield, where she grew up. There she met and married Abija Prince, an ex-slave who had gained his freedom after serving in the French and Indian War.

Shortly after they were married, Abijah Prince purchased Lucy's freedom, and the two of them moved to a farm in Guilford, Vermont. Eventually, they had six children; two of their sons fought in the revolutionary war. Abijah Prince also became one of the fifty-five original founders of the town of Sunderland in Vermont.

Two years after the American Revolution, a wealthy neighbor tried to force the Princes off their land. Abijah Prince was then almost eighty years old, so Lucy Prince, twenty-five years younger than her husband, rode across Vermont to seek the aid of the governor's council. Fortunately, the council sided with the Princes and ordered the neighbor to leave them alone.

In 1794 her husband died. For the next eighteen years she rode horseback over the mountains to visit his grave.

It was shortly after his death that another neighbor tried to claim some of the Princes' property. Again Lucy fought back, this time taking her case all the way to the Vermont Supreme Court. After ruling in her favor, the judge told her that she had made one of the most convincing arguments he had ever heard.

Lucy Terry Prince, America's first poet of African descent, died in 1821 at the age of eighty-eight. The remarkable sixteen-year-old girl who had written "The Bar's Fight" certainly turned out to be a courageous fighter herself.

Jean Baptiste Pointe DuSable

Frontier Trader, Fur-trapper
1745-1818

Chicago is the third largest urban center in the United States. It was a black man named Jean Baptiste Pointe DuSable who first put the city on the map.

It is generally believed that DuSable was born in Saint-Dominique (Haiti) in about 1745 to an African woman and a French merchant-sailor. After working for a time as a seaman on his father's ships, DuSable's father took him to France to be educated. There he developed a love for European art. At one time he may have owned several art treasures.

When DuSable returned from France, he traveled to New Orleans. Then, working as a trapper and fur trader, he made his way up the Mississippi River to St. Louis.

At the time, England, Spain, and France were all trying to gain control of the new territories in America. When the British took over the city of St. Louis, they began restricting people of French background. So DuSable moved further north to Peoria, Illinois.

In 1769, while on a trip to Canada, DuSable stopped at a place the Indians called "Checagou." Recognizing the unique advantages offered by Checagou's location, he set up a trading post on the marshy shores of the river. His instincts were right. Checagou later flourished and became known as Chicago. Today, it is one of the greatest centers of trade and commerce in the world.

DuSable's trading post prospered, in part, because he was able to speak English, French, Spanish, and several Indian dialects. More importantly, he had developed a special relationship with various Indian groups living in the Illinois territory. His remarkable ability to work with diverse groups and to interest them in his business venture added to his success.

Before long, the post expanded and included a horse stable, workshop, bakery, dairy, smokehouse, barn, and several other buildings. Within a short time, it became the main supply station for trappers, traders, and Indians and was the key route for merchant trading in Detroit and Canada. Among the many things he supplied were furs, meats, wheat, and bread.

Although DuSable had become a successful trader, his French background continued to cause him problems, and he was arrested twice because of it. Yet, the British governor, Patrick Sinclair, was so impressed with DuSable's abilities that he asked him to take charge of a settlement on the St. Clair River. DuSable did so, and, at the same time, acquired considerable property in Peoria.

In 1784 DuSable returned to Chicago with his wife Catherine, who was a Potawatomi Indian, and their children. Then in 1800, for reasons unknown, he sold his Chicago properties for only $1,200 and moved to St. Charles, Missouri, where his granddaughter lived. He died there in 1818, almost penniless, and was buried in St. Charles Borromeo Cemetery.

Although he was not honored during his lifetime, Jean Baptiste Pointe DuSable, successful trader and entrepreneur, had laid the foundation for one of the largest and most important cities of the world.

Crispus Attucks

Mariner, Patriot
1723-1770

The first to defy and the first to die...." So read a line of poetry about Crispus Attucks who, with four other men, was shot to death during a fight with British soldiers in the Massachusetts Colony in 1770. Later, the fight became known as the Boston Massacre.

Born a slave of African and Natick Indian heritage, Attucks ran away from his owner, William Brown of Framingham, Massachusetts, when he was twenty-seven years old. He signed on as a sailor on a departing boat and spent the next twenty years of his life working on cargo and whaling ships. While at sea, he taught himself to read and write.

The rough, free life of a sailor suited Attucks. He was strong, brave, and quick to take the lead in difficult situations, especially those that threatened his freedom or the freedom of others. It was quite natural for him, therefore, to side with Boston colonists when they refused to obey England's oppressive laws and restrictions.

In Boston, the situation had become so tense that the British stationed troops there to keep the colonists under control. Since 1765 there had been numerous scuffles and fights between British soldiers and American patriots. Tensions mounted. Then on March 5, 1770, what began as a minor scuffle became a major incident on the road to revolution.

Hugh Montgomery, a British soldier who was standing guard outside the Custom House, struck a young boy who had insulted him. The boy, holding his injured head, ran crying through the streets. Immediately, an angry crowd, led by Attucks, appeared and threatened Montgomery. They began pelting him with snowballs and pieces of ice. Soon, twelve more soldiers from the British Twenty-ninth Regiment appeared, armed with muskets and bayonets.

When the crowd saw the soldiers, they hesitated. But Attucks charged ahead waving a heavy stick. "Don't be afraid. Knock 'em over. They dare not fire," he cried. Unfortunately, he was wrong. Faced with the angry crowd, the soldiers panicked. In desperation they fired into the mob, killing Crispus Attucks and Samuel Grey instantly and wounding nine other men, three of whom died.

Public reaction seesawed between shock and anger. Attucks's body lay in state in Boston's Faneuil Hall for three days. Thousands attended his funeral and all shops in the city closed. Seven British soldiers and their commander were tried for murder but exonerated.

The Boston Massacre marked a major turning point in the events leading to the American Revolution. As John Adams later wrote: "On that night, the foundations of American Independence were laid." It is noteworthy that those "foundations" rested in part on the courage and leadership of a runaway slave named Crispus Attucks.

Sketch from a book published in 1855: *The Colored Patriots of the American Revolution*

Benjamin Banneker

Inventor, Surveyor, Mathematician, Astronomer
1731-1806

"The color of the skin is in no way connected with strength of the mind or intellectual powers." **— Benjamin Banneker**

He constructed the first clock built in the United States, predicted a solar eclipse, and helped design the city of Washington, D.C.

Benjamin Banneker was born on November 9, 1731, on a farm near Baltimore, Maryland. His grandmother, Molly Walsh, was an Englishwoman and former indentured servant. She acquired some land and bought an African slave named Banneka (or Bannka), whom she married. Their daughter, Mary, following her mother's example, purchased and married a slave named Robert. Mary and Robert adopted the family name, Bannak (later changed to Banneker), and acquired a farm of their own.

Using an old Bible, Molly Walsh taught Benjamin to read and write. At age twelve he began attending a nearby Quaker school, where he showed a strong interest in mathematics. In fact, he often made up math problems just for the fun of solving them.

When Banneker was about nineteen, he met Josef Levi, a traveling salesman, who showed him a pocket watch. Banneker had never seen one before and was fascinated. When he got home, he drew up plans and made the necessary calculations to make one himself. Two years later, it was finished. Made entirely of wood, each gear had been carved by hand. It kept perfect time for more than forty years.

By the time of the American Revolution, Banneker had begun a serious study of astronomy. Quickly mastering the science, he predicted a solar eclipse for April 14, 1789. Two leading astronomers disagreed with his calculations, but Banneker's prediction was correct.

In 1792 Banneker began publishing an almanac. In addition to listing holidays and eclipses, it provided weather and medical information, the hours of sunrise and sunset, and a tide table for the Chesapeake Bay. His almanacs also included poems and antislavery essays.

When the decision was made to move the nation's capital from Philadelphia to Washington, D.C., in 1791, President Washington appointed Banneker to the civil engineering team that was planning the layout of the new city. The team was headed by Pierre Charles L'Enfant, a young Frenchman. A year later, L'Enfant quit and returned to France with all the plans. For a while it looked as if a year's work would be lost. But Banneker reproduced them from memory.

Although Banneker was preoccupied with matters of mathematics and astronomy, he also was concerned about the condition of blacks throughout the country. In 1791 he wrote a letter to Thomas Jefferson, criticizing his statement that "blacks were inferior to whites," and included a copy of his almanac to prove his point. Jefferson quickly changed his opinion and sent a copy of the almanac to the French Academy of Sciences in Paris. Banneker's almanac also was shown in Britain's House of Commons to support the argument that blacks could be educated.

In addition to his work in mathematics and astronomy, Banneker proposed that the U.S. government establish a Department of Peace. He also advocated free public education for all children and the elimination of the death penalty.

On October 25, 1806, Benjamin Banneker, the man who had built the first clock in the United States, died. He had been ahead of his time in more ways than one.

Phillis Wheatley

Poet
1753-1784

Should you, my lord, while you peruse my song,
Wonder from whence my love of Freedom
    sprung,
Whence flow these wishes for the common good,
By feeling hearts alone best understood,
I, young in life, by seeming cruel fate
Was snatch'd from Afric's fancy'd happy seat.[2]

Those are the words of Phillis Wheatley, a young, African-born woman who was kidnapped by slave traders when she was about eight years old and brought to Boston, Massachusetts, in 1761. There she was bought by John Wheatley, a wealthy merchant tailor, as a lady's maid for his wife Susannah.

A small, frail child, Phillis was well cared for. She was assigned chores that she was able to do. Very intelligent, she learned English quickly and was taught to read. When she was fourteen, she began writing poetry. Her first work to receive widespread attention was "An Elegiac Poem, on the Death of that Celebrated Divine. . .George Whitefield." It was printed in Boston in 1770.

Phillis Wheatley was never very strong. When her health began to fail in 1772, the Wheatleys freed her and sent her to England. While she was there, she impressed several members of the nobility. They arranged for her book, *Poems on Various Subjects, Religious and Moral*, to be published. Many prominent Massachusetts men (including John Hancock) signed the foreword of her book.

Arrangements were made for Ms. Wheatley to be introduced to the king and queen of England. But before the meeting could take place, she received word that Mrs. Wheatley was ill, so she quickly returned to America.

When Mrs. Wheatley died in 1774, Ms. Wheatley remained with the family and kept house for John Wheatley. She continued to write, and, in 1775, dedicated a poem to George Washington, which appeared in Thomas Paine's *Pennsylvania Magazine*. Washington was so impressed that he invited her to visit him at his headquarters in Cambridge, Massachusetts.

After the death of John Wheatley in 1778, Ms. Wheatley was forced to move from the house where she had grown up. Shortly thereafter, she married a man named John Peters. He was frequently away, and the marriage was unhappy. Although in ill health, Phillis Wheatley had to work as a servant to support herself.

Two of her three children died shortly after they were born. Then on December 5, 1784, she passed away at age thirty-one. Her third child died the same day.

Phillis Wheatley is remembered today because of her role in the development of black American literature. Her sensitive poetry proved at the time that blacks, when given the opportunity, were equal to whites, both intellectually and emotionally. At a time when the fight against slavery often seemed endless, Phillis Wheatley's poems provided both hope and ammunition.

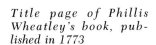

Title page of Phillis Wheatley's book, published in 1773

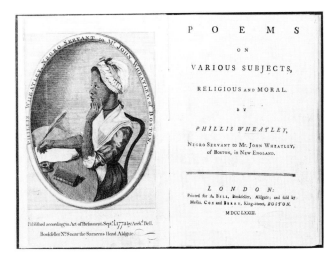

Peter Salem

American Revolutionary War Soldier
1750-1816

"We hold these truths to be self-evident, that all men are created equal...." This statement comes from the Declaration of Independence, and to thousands of black revolutionary war soldiers like Peter Salem, it was more than just pretty words; it was a promise they expected the new nation to remember.

In June 1775, 1,500 Americans faced two to three thousand British redcoats at the famous Battle of Bunker Hill. Three times the British charged. Twice they were forced back. The third time, the British commander, Major John Pitcairn, pressed forward shouting, "The day is ours." Those were his last words, for it was then that Peter Salem, a black American soldier, shot him in the chest, killing him. The British won the fight when the American's ammunition ran out, but by then it didn't matter. The American Revolution was under way.

Peter Salem almost missed the battle of Bunker Hill. Because many whites feared slave rebellions, it was decided in May 1775 that only free blacks would be accepted as soldiers. Although Salem had fought earlier at Concord and Lexington, under the new ruling, he was not allowed to serve in the American army. Some slaves were freed, however, so they could fight. Peter Salem was one of them. Once free, he immediately enlisted in Colonel Nixon's Fifth Massachusetts Regiment—just in time to fight at Bunker Hill in June.

Soon, even free black fighters made some whites uneasy. So under pressure from the Continental Congress, General George Washington issued an order that banned all black soldiers from fighting. The British decided to take advantage of the situation and offered freedom to all slaves willing to fight for England. When Washington heard about England's offer, he immediately reversed his decision and allowed blacks to enlist in January 1776. As a result, more than 5,000 blacks volunteered their services. In fact, black soldiers are known to have fought in every major battle of the revolutionary war.

Many slaves who fought in the revolutionary war were freed by their owners who had taken the words of the Declaration of Independence to heart. These black soldiers fought bravely, hoping that slavery would be abolished throughout the colonies. They fought not only for their own freedom but also for that of their families and friends. Their efforts were not totally in vain. By the end of the war, over 60,000 slaves had been set free—some because they had joined the fighting, others because many northern states had outlawed slavery by this time.

Peter Salem fought not only at Concord, Lexington, and Bunker Hill but also at Saratoga and Stony Point. He remained in the Continental Army until about 1780 and then settled down in Leicester, Massachusetts. In 1816 he died in a Framingham poorhouse.

James Forten

Abolitionist, Businessman
1766-1842

"I'm a prisoner here for the liberties of my country. I never, never shall prove a traitor to her interests." Those were the words of James Forten, a young powder boy who was serving aboard an American ship when it was captured by the British during the revolutionary war.

Born free in Philadelphia, James went to work in a grocery store to help support his family after the death of his father. When he was fifteen, he persuaded his mother to let him sign on as a powder boy aboard the American ship *Royal Louis*. On its second cruise, the *Royal Louis* was captured by the British ship *Amphyon*.

In those days, black prisoners of war usually were sold by the British to work on plantations in the West Indies. But James was lucky. Another boy, the captain's son, was also aboard the *Amphyon*. After playing a game of marbles, the two became friends. The captain offered to take James back to England and set him free, if he would renounce his country. Without hesitating, James refused.

Not wanting to sell the boy into slavery, the captain transferred James to the prison ship *Jersey*, anchored off Long Island, New York. For the next seven months, he lived in the hold of the filthy, overcrowded ship. He ate moldy bread and spoiled meat and watched other prisoners die. Once, he had a chance to escape by hiding inside the trunk of an American officer who was being exchanged for a British prisoner. But James let a younger boy take his place.

When James Forten finally was set free in a prisoner exchange, he walked home to Philadelphia from New York. In 1786 he took a job as an apprentice to Robert Bridges, a sailmaker. Two years later, after becoming foreman, Forten was managing forty workers, many of whom were white.

When Bridges died in 1798, Forten took over the business and developed it into one of the most prosperous in Philadelphia. Partly because of a sailmaking device he had invented, which made it easier to handle heavy sails, he soon amassed a fortune of over $100,000.

A respected and influential businessman, Forten used his wealth to fight slavery and improve the conditions of poor blacks. His writings, published in a pamphlet called *A Series of Letters by a Man of Color*, helped defeat antiblack legislation in 1813.

Always a patriot, he recruited blacks to defend Philadelphia against a British invasion during the war of 1812. And he protested efforts to resettle free blacks in Africa.

Although James Forten died in 1842, before slavery was outlawed in the United States, he never gave up hope that it would end one day. "The spirit of Freedom is marching with rapid strides and causing tyrants to tremble," he said. "May America awake...."

Drawing of the British prison ship *Jersey* by John Trumbull

James Armistead

American Revolutionary War Spy
1760-1832

The bravery shown by Crispus Attucks in the Boston Massacre helped bring about the American Revolution; but it was the courage of another man, James Armistead, that helped bring the revolutionary war to a successful conclusion.

James Armistead was twenty-one years old when his master, William Armistead from New Kent County, Virginia, gave him permission to serve with the American army in the revolutionary war. He was assigned to assist the Marquis de Lafayette, a young French general who had volunteered to fight with the Americans.

In 1791 Lafayette headed a small, ragged army of about 1,200 men in Virginia. His orders were to bring pressure on two British armies: one led by Lord Charles Cornwallis, and the other under the command of Benedict Arnold, the American who had turned traitor and joined the British. At the time, almost the entire state of Virginia was under British control.

Because Lafayette's tattered troops weren't strong enough to meet the British in a full-scale battle, Lafayette was forced to tag along behind the redcoats and engage them in small skirmishes. While following the British, Lafayette received orders from George Washington to find out what the enemy was planning for the coming months. Immediately, he assigned James Armistead to go undercover as a spy.

Armistead appeared at Benedict Arnold's headquarters shortly afterwards and offered his services as a servant and a guide. In return, Armistead asked to be freed when the British won the war. Arnold agreed. Quickly gaining their trust, Armistead began sending secret reports back to Lafayette detailing British positions. When Benedict Arnold was reassigned, James Armistead established himself in a similar position with Lord Cornwallis.

In April Cornwallis suddenly disappeared with his troops. But James Armistead was able to provide Americans with his location— Yorktown on the York River by the Chesapeake Bay. This was the news Lafayette had been waiting for. He joined forces with Washington's troops, and together they set out to trap the British between the American army on land and the French fleet anchored in Chesapeake Bay. The plan worked. Cornwallis was surrounded. On October 19, 1781, after ten days of fighting and negotiating, the British surrendered.

As a reward for his services, Armistead was freed by the General Assembly of Virginia and later granted a yearly pension of $40 for the rest of his life. He changed his last name to Lafayette in recognition of his friendship with his former commander. General Lafayette, in turn, became active in efforts to abolish slavery and obtain equal rights for blacks.

The American Revolution ended with the Battle of Yorktown—an American victory that was due in part to the valuable intelligence work of James Armistead.

Elizabeth Freeman

Abolitionist
1742-1829

It took the entire U.S. Army to destroy slavery in the South but only a determined black woman to end it in Massachusetts.

Elizabeth Freeman grew up at a time when the American colonies were becoming more and more dissatisfied with British rule. In 1776 the Declaration of Independence was written, and everyone was talking about freedom, liberty, and equality. The home of Colonel John Ashley, where Elizabeth Freeman and her sisters were slaves, was no different.

As Ms. Freeman served meals to the Ashley family, she listened to the discussions and drew a few conclusions of her own. Many people did not feel that the new ideas about equality applied to slaves, but Ms. Freeman did. And once the revolutionary war ended in October 1781, she decided to take action. She left the Ashley household and refused to return.

Elizabeth Freeman approached a young lawyer named Theodore Sedgwick and asked him to help her gain her freedom. Sedgwick listened with interest as she argued that, according to the Declaration of Independence and the new Massachusetts Constitution adopted in 1780, she should be free. Convinced that they had a case, Sedgwick decided to represent her.

In 1781 Ms. Freeman's case was heard by the county court in Great Barrington, Massachusetts. There she claimed that, as a result of the American Revolution, slavery was illegal and she should not have to return to the Ashley household. The jury agreed. Elizabeth Freeman was given her freedom, and the judge ordered Colonel Ashley to pay her thirty shillings in damages.

After her victory, Ms. Freeman went to work for the Sedgwick family. She died on December 28, 1829. As a result of her court battle, she was freed, and slavery in the state of Massachusetts ended. Elizabeth Freeman, a woman who had spent her life waiting on tables, had served up a major lesson to the slaveholders of Massachusetts.

Signing of the Declaration of Independence, from a painting by John Trumbull

Richard Allen

Bishop, Abolitionist
1760-1831

"We were stolen from our mother country and brought here. We have tilled the ground and made fortunes for thousands. . . ."
— Richard Allen

One morning in November 1787, Richard Allen and two friends, Absalom Jones and William White, were pulled from their knees while praying in St. George's Methodist Episcopal Church in Philadelphia and told that, because they were black, they must stay in the rear of the gallery. Rather than do this, the three men walked out, followed by the other black members of the congregation.

Richard Allen was born a slave in Philadelphia but was sold along with his family to a Mr. Stockley in Dover, Delaware. While living with the Stockleys, Allen taught himself to read and write and began to attend Methodist church meetings. Working as a day laborer and bricklayer, he managed to save enough money to purchase his freedom in 1783.

For the next few years, Allen traveled with a Methodist minister and occasionally was allowed to preach to mixed congregations. Returning to Philadelphia in 1786, he began holding prayer meetings for black congregations. Shortly afterward, the incident at St. George's took place.

Following the walkout, Allen and Jones organized the Free African Society, a self-help group that opposed slavery, and laid plans for the construction of an all-black church. Their plans were interrupted, however, when a serious yellow fever epidemic hit Philadelphia, killing hundreds of people. Allen and Jones arranged for members of the city's black community to serve as nurses and undertakers.

After the epidemic had run its course, Allen continued with his plans for a black church. Working as a shoemaker, he saved enough money to buy a lot and begin construction. On July 17, 1794, the Bethel African Methodist Episcopal Church was founded.

In 1816 Bethel cut its ties to the Methodist Church. By uniting Bethel with other African Methodist churches, Allen helped create the African Methodist Episcopal Church (AME). He became its first bishop. Eventually, it would include thousands of members throughout the country and become a national organization.

In 1795 Richard Allen opened a school for black children. He also led the black community in petitioning the Pennsylvania legislature to abolish slavery. And when the British threatened to invade Philadelphia in 1812, he and Absalom Jones helped raise 2,500 black troops to defend the city.

Because of the courage and vision of men like Richard Allen, churches became a vital part of black life in the United States. They provided a training ground for black leaders and unified the efforts of the black community to oppose slavery and racial discrimination. This tradition of community involvement continues today.

During the civil rights movement of the 1950s and 1960s, black ministers and their congregations took the lead in supporting efforts to end racial segregation. As a result, many black churches were dynamited or firebombed. Yet, the black church has always prevailed—thanks in part to men like Richard Allen.

Paul Cuffe

Mariner, Merchant, Humanitarian
1759-1817

Though he fought hard for the rights of black people in America, in his heart, Paul Cuffe thought they could be free only in Africa. Born in 1759, on Cuttyhunk Island in Massachusetts, Paul Cuffe was the son of a former slave and a woman from the Wampanoag Indian tribe. At sixteen, he turned to the sea for his living and, eventually, became wealthy from fishing, whaling, and shipping. He became a part or full owner of at least ten ships and traveled to Europe, Africa, Canada, and the Caribbean.

But his wealth could not protect him from racial discrimination. In 1778 the Massachusetts Constitution denied blacks and American Indians the right to vote. As a result, Captain Paul Cuffe refused to pay his taxes. He and other blacks petitioned the Massachusetts government to restore their voting rights; they pointed out that many blacks and American Indians were fighting alongside Americans in the revolutionary war. A Massachusetts court honored their petition and granted all free, tax-paying blacks the right to vote in 1783.

Cuffe was also concerned about the right of children to obtain an education. When the town of Westport refused to build a school, he built one on his own farm and donated it to the community.

The failure of the American Revolution to end slavery everywhere in the colonies, and the racial discrimination he and other blacks continued to face, convinced Paul Cuffe that they must look to Africa for their freedom. This was not a new idea. Several black leaders agreed with him that America would never change and that a black state in Africa was the only answer.

In 1810 Cuffe traveled to Sierra Leone, Africa, with the idea of establishing a colony of Afro-Americans that would be supported by trade with the United States. In December 1815, he sponsored a second trip—this time accompanied by thirty-eight blacks (including twenty children) who planned to settle.

Within a few years of Paul Cuffe's settlement in Africa, the American Colonization Society was formed. Its leaders, however, were not black people, but slaveholders. They favored the emigration of free blacks to Africa, thinking that if free blacks were gone the pressure they exerted to end slavery would be gone, too.

The American Colonization Society persuaded Congress to acquire territory in Africa where American blacks could settle. The new country was called Liberia (after the word "liberty"), and its capital was called Monrovia after President James Monroe.

Over the next thirty years, approximately 14,000 black people returned to Africa. Some were free blacks. Others were slaves who were freed under the condition that they leave the United States. Still others were Africans who had been freed from illegal slave ships.

Many more blacks—certainly many slaves—would have emigrated to Africa had they been able to. But many black leaders, including James Forten, Richard Allen, and Absalom Jones, opposed the idea. They believed that if free blacks left, it would be a betrayal of their slave brothers left behind. Also, they argued that black people had helped build America and they were entitled to all the benefits, including freedom, that America had to offer.

Paul Cuffe, sometimes referred to as the Father of the Black Back-to-Africa Movement in the United States, also was instrumental in gaining rights for blacks in Massachusetts. He was a remarkable businessman and humanitarian.

Gabriel Prosser

Slave Insurrectionist
1776-1800

Of the hundreds of slave uprisings that occurred in the United States, one of the most important was led by a twenty-four-year-old man named Gabriel Prosser. It took place in 1800 and was known as The Great Gabriel Conspiracy. With his brothers, Martin and Solomon, and more than 1,000 slave followers, Prosser organized the revolt, obtained weapons, and worked out the final details of the plot.

Prosser's idea was to seize Richmond and, thereby, encourage slave uprisings all over Virginia and the South. The slaves planned to meet on August 30 in Old Brook Swamp, six miles from the city. There they would divide into three groups: one group would attack the armory, another would take the powder house, and the third would set fires to divert attention from the others.

But on that Saturday night, a huge storm arose, destroying roads, wiping out bridges, and making travel impossible. Brook Swamp was flooded, and only a few hundred slaves were able to get to the meeting place. Meanwhile, two slaves became frightened and confessed the plot. Governor James Monroe placed Richmond on full alert and sent troops to apprehend Prosser and his men.

As the full plan became known, panic swept over the city. About forty slaves were executed during the next few weeks. Prosser was captured and questioned. But in spite of numerous beatings, he refused to name any of his followers. Tried and condemned to hang, Gabriel Prosser went to his death in silence on October 7, 1800.

York
Explorer, Scout, Interpreter
1770-1832

In 1803 President Thomas Jefferson authorized the purchase of 875,000 square miles of unexplored territory. The new land, which was previously owned by France, became known as the Louisiana Purchase. It stretched from Louisiana in the south to Canada in the north and from the Mississippi River in the east to the Rocky Mountains in the west. Eventually, thirteen states would be carved from it. Its acquisition would double the size of the United States and open up the West to settlement.

Since no one knew what lay in this vast land, Congress authorized a special expedition under the leadership of Meriwether Lewis and William Clark to explore it. President Thomas Jefferson wanted to determine a land route to the Pacific Ocean.

In the spring of 1804, the expedition started out. Among the forty-five men and one woman in the party was a twenty-three-year-old man named York. He was William Clark's personal slave and friend since childhood. Standing more than six feet tall and weighing more than 200 pounds, York was an imposing figure. He was strong, athletic, and a successful hunter with an extensive knowledge of woodlore. Because he was able to speak some French and several Indian languages, he also served as an interpreter when it became necessary.

The expedition was guided by a French trapper named Toussaint Charbonneau. His wife, a Shoshone Indian woman named Sacajawea or "Bird Woman," was a translator. When the expedition met with Indians, Sacajawea would tell her husband what they were saying. He, in turn, would repeat it in French to York, and York would translate the French into English for Lewis and Clark.

Indians were fascinated by York. Most had never seen a man of his size, skin color, and agility. Flathead Indians thought he had painted himself with charcoal as their warriors did when they were victorious in battle. In one Mandan village, Indians tried to rub his skin to see if the color would come off. Because of their interest in him, York was assigned the task of trading with them for food and horses.

The expedition reached the Pacific Ocean at the mouth of the Columbia River in November 1805, then returned to St. Louis, Missouri, on September 23, 1806. The members of the party faced incredible hardships during their two-and-a-half year journey. In all, they traveled more than 8,000 miles through territory that is now the states of Missouri, Nebraska, Kansas, Montana, Idaho, Iowa, Washington, Oregon, and North and South Dakota. They were the first people to cross the North American continent to the Pacific Ocean and to bring back vital information about the terrain, the plants and animals, and the location of Indian tribes.

After the expedition, Clark freed York, who returned to Kentucky to be near his wife, a slave of a local family. York's skills as a scout and an interpreter contributed to the success of the historic Lewis and Clark expedition. The Louisiana Purchase had cost the U.S. government about fifteen million dollars. York's presence helped insure that it was money well spent.

Denmark Vesey

Slave Insurrectionist
1767-1822

I n 1799 a slave named Denmark Vesey won $1,500 with a lottery ticket and used $600 of it to pay for his freedom. In 1822 he tried to gain the freedom of every slave in Charleston, South Carolina. This time he paid with his life.

For almost twenty years, Denmark Vesey had been the property of a sea captain named Joseph Vesey. When he finally bought his freedom, Vesey set up his own carpentry shop and gradually became wealthy from it. He was outspoken about the evils of slavery, frequently encouraging slaves and free blacks to stand up for their rights. Finally, he decided the time had come for action. In 1821 he planned a massive slave revolt that would allow them to take their freedom by force.

Denmark Vesey selected the leaders for his revolt carefully: Peter Poyas, cool, courageous, and a born organizer; Gullah Jack, an African-born magic man, feared and respected by many slaves; and Ned and Rolla Bennett, slaves belonging to the governor of the state. Secretly, Vesey organized his strike force. (Eventually, it would grow to include 9,000 followers.)

He planned the revolt for Sunday, July 14, 1822. His army would move at midnight, striking various key points in the city. But his plan was never carried out. A house slave who had been asked to join the revolt betrayed it instead. Because of Vesey's secret method of operation, however, the house slave did not know the names of the leaders of the revolt. But he knew enough. Charleston city officials acted quickly.

When Vesey heard they had been betrayed, he changed the date of the uprising to June 16. But it was too late. Another slave had gone to the authorities and confessed. Fearing capture, Vesey went into hiding but was arrested on June 22. Five days later, he was tried and convicted; the judge handed down the death sentence.

On July 2, 1822, at 6:00 A.M., Denmark Vesey was hanged along with Peter Poyas and four other followers. Eventually, thirty-seven other blacks were put to death for taking part in the revolt. For Denmark Vesey, personal freedom had not been enough. He gave his life so that others could be free.

Vesey was inspired by Toussaint L'Ouverture's successful revolt in Haiti.

Slave Uprisings

In 1811 between 300 and 500 slaves revolted in St. John the Baptist Parish in the Louisiana Territory. Flying their own flag and armed with axes, spears, and other homemade weapons, they marched in military fashion into New Orleans. Their leader was Charles Deslandes. Although the slaves were well organized and well disciplined, they were no match for the army troops commanded by Wade Hampton, and their revolt quickly fell apart.

Very little is known of the Louisiana slave rebellion in spite of the fact that it was the largest to be carried out in U.S. territory; The revolts of Gabriel Prosser and Denmark Vesey, while involving larger numbers, were stopped before they had a chance to begin.

Much more shocking was the slave uprising that took place in Stono, South Carolina, in 1739, just twenty miles outside the city of Charleston. It started when slaves, under the leadership of a man named Jemmy, killed two men guarding a warehouse containing guns and ammunition and began a revolt that lasted several days.

Slave rebellions were not uncommon in the states, but they were never as big or as bloody as revolts in the Caribbean. In 1522 a slave uprising occurred on the island of Hispaniola. Later, revolts followed in Puerto Rico, Jamaica, Cuba, Martinique, Barbados, St. Vincent, Antigua, and the Virgin Islands. In 1789 a slave named Toussaint L'Ouverture led a revolt in Haiti that not only brought an end to slavery there but also ended French control of the island. Toussaint L'Ouverture's success later inspired the revolts of Gabriel Prosser in Virginia and Denmark Vesey in South Carolina.

One reason for the greater frequency of revolts in the Caribbean is that, in the islands, slaves greatly outnumbered the white population.

Slaves who rebelled and lost were generally sentenced to death. But slave uprisings and the threat of slave uprisings continued both in the United States and in the Caribbean until slavery itself had been wiped out.

Garcia
Soldier

In the years before Florida became a state, the territory was a haven for hundreds of runaway slaves who settled among the Indians and established small communities. One such settlement, Fort Negro, sheltered close to 300 men, women, and children of black, Seminole, or mixed ancestry. The fort was protected by men under the command of a man named Garcia.

Built originally by the British on the Apalachicola River some sixty miles from the Georgia border, Fort Negro had been taken over by black settlers when the British withdrew after the War of 1812. The fort quickly became a symbol of freedom to slaves in the southern states, and many ran away hoping to find safety there.

Concerned that Fort Negro was posing a threat to southern slaveholders, U.S. General Andrew Jackson, commander of the Seventh Military, decided to destroy it. Although Florida belonged to Spain at the time, and an attack on Fort Negro would be considered an invasion of a foreign territory, Jackson ordered it anyway.

On the morning of July 27, 1816, a large U.S. military force approached Fort Negro and ordered Garcia to surrender. Garcia refused. The fort was well built and the men defending it were well armed. So the attackers heated cannonballs and fired them over the walls. One landed on the powderhouse and set off an explosion that was heard for miles. More than 200 people were killed or wounded. Garcia was taken prisoner and shot by a firing squad. The remaining sixty-three survivors were returned north to slavery.

Black Seminoles

The destruction of Fort Negro in 1816 marked the beginning of the Seminole Wars, a series of three Indian wars that were to stretch over forty years and cost the U.S. government more than thirty million dollars.

Although the conflict is named for the Seminole Indians, it was, in the words of General Sidney Thomas Jesup, ". . . a Negro and not an Indian War." The Seminoles had long offered protection to escaped slaves, and, over the years, thousands of runaway blacks had settled among them. Often, they intermarried and became active in tribal affairs.

Most distressing to the slaveholders was the fact that runaways would often band together and, with Indian help, return later to raid Georgia plantations in an effort to free friends and relatives. In an effort to stop this practice, slaveholders brought pressure on the U.S. government to take control of Florida, recapture the runaway slaves, and end the threat to their plantations. In 1819 Spain ceded Florida to the United States in exchange for five million dollars worth of claims that American citizens held against Spain. Still, resistance among the Seminoles and their black allies remained strong. Although greatly outnumbered, they continued to engage in hit-and-run guerrilla warfare, eventually taking the lives of 1,500 U.S. soldiers. However, in 1823 the Seminoles were forced to accept a treaty restricting them to reservations in southern Florida.

From the beginning, black men such as Abraham, John Caesar, and John Horse served as important advisers and negotiators for Seminole chiefs.

Abraham, an escaped slave, advised Seminole Chief Micanopy. He accompanied him to Washington, D.C., in 1825 and later helped negotiate the Treaty of Fort Gibson.

In 1835 the Second Seminole War broke out when the black wife of Chief Osceola was kidnapped by a government agent and sold into slavery. Blacks were heavily involved in the conflict. When

General Jesup's troops overran an Indian camp in 1837, they captured fifty-five members of Osceola's personal bodyguard. Of these, fifty-two were black. Once again, Abraham took a leading role in both military and diplomatic activities. Partly because of his negotiations, the Seminoles agreed to the 1837 Treaty of Fort Dade and left Florida for Indian Territory in Oklahoma.

John Caesar had lived among the Seminoles most of his life and was an adviser to King Phillip (Emathla), the second chief of the Seminole Nation after Micanopy. Caesar took the lead in encouraging resistance among the plantation slaves in the St. Johns River area. Because of his influence, the U.S. government agreed to allow blacks to move west with their Seminole allies. Although this guaranteed the freedom of many escaped slaves, it also reduced the danger of general slave uprisings on Florida and Georgia plantations.

John Horse, a black Indian, was a signer of the Treaty of Fort Dade. When the United States violated the treaty, he joined Osceola in renewing hostilities. While meeting with U.S. Army officials under a flag of truce, Horse, Osceola, Wild Cat, and other Seminole leaders were taken prisoner and jailed. Together with Wild Cat, Horse led a daring mass prison escape. Chased by a force of nearly 1,000 men, they evaded capture and defeated the American army led by Colonel Zachary Taylor at the Battle of Lake Okeechobee. Later, John Horse led a group of black Seminoles into Mexico, where they were allowed to settle in return for guarding the border against rustlers and bandits.

Ironically, the U.S. Army, which had spent more than forty years fighting the black Seminoles, hired many of them after the Civil War. In fact, three black Seminoles later won the Congressional Medal of Honor. Long considered the best hunters, trackers, scouts, and fighters in the business, the black Seminoles were a major force in bringing law and order to the Texas-Mexican border.

Nat Turner

Slave Insurrectionist
1800-1831

"I would never be of any service to anyone as a slave"—Nat Turner

In February 1831, there was an eclipse of the sun. A man in Southampton County, Virginia, by the name of Nat Turner, took it as a sign from God that he should lead a huge slave uprising to free those held in bondage.

Gathering together his closest friends, Turner made plans for a revolt that would take place on the Fourth of July. As the day approached, however, he became ill. Canceling the plans, the men waited for another sign. On August 13, 1831, a bluish-green haze covered the sun. Interpreting this as the sign they had been waiting for, Turner and six followers met again to work out the final details of the uprising.

On August 22, the revolt began. The first house to be attacked belonged to Nat Turner's owner, Joseph Travis. Travis, his wife and child, and two other people were killed. For forty hours the revolt continued. Between sixty and eighty slaves joined the rebellion. They killed at least fifty-seven slaveholders and their families, sparing only poor whites who did not own slaves.

When word of the unexpected revolt reached the authorities, hundreds of armed white men rode off in search of Nat Turner. Dozens of rebel slaves, carrying only a few weapons, were killed or captured. Turner evaded authorities for two months. Finally, on October 30, 1831, the Virginia militia captured him. On November 5, he was tried, found guilty, and sentenced to death. Six days later he was hanged and his body was disposed of secretly.

Although the revolt was over, reaction to it was just beginning. Of those formally charged with participating in the uprising, twenty-four were either acquitted or freed for lack of evidence. Twenty-nine were convicted; seventeen of these, including Nat Turner, were hanged. Approximately 200 other blacks were killed by slave owners who were determined to terrify the remaining black population into submission.

The white community was shocked by the revolt. They could not believe that Nat Turner, of all people, had led it. Far from having a reputation as a violent or difficult slave, Turner had been a deeply religious man. Known as "The Prophet," he had preached on Sundays and was highly respected by both black and white communities.

Nat Turner went to his death with dignity and courage. He had said that on the day he was to die, the sun would refuse to shine as a sign from God that slavery was evil. Not everyone took Nat Turner's religious pronouncements seriously, but the local sheriff did. He refused to cut the rope that would spring the trap on the gallows. No one else was anxious to do it either, so an old drunk was brought from forty miles away to act as executioner. While the sun didn't exactly refuse to shine, the sky did go dark when a major thunderstorm arose on the day of the hanging. Thunderstorms in November are a bit unusual, and many people were quite impressed by the occurrence.

Joseph Cinque

African Patriot
1817-1879

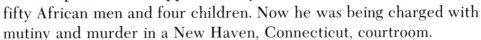

"**G**ive us free. Give us free." Though he spoke very little English, there was no doubt as to what Joseph Cinque wanted. He had seized control of a slave ship and freed approximately fifty African men and four children. Now he was being charged with mutiny and murder in a New Haven, Connecticut, courtroom.

The story began when Cinque was kidnapped by slave traders in 1839 and sold to the owner of a slave factory at Lomboko on the African coast. From there, he was shipped to Havana, Cuba, on a Portuguese slave ship under conditions so terrible that half the slaves aboard died.

It was illegal to bring new slaves into Cuba at the time, so upon their arrival in Havana, Cinque and the rest of the slave "cargo" were sold secretly to a planter named Ruiz. Together with another slave-owner named Montes, Ruiz transferred the slaves to a ship called the *Amistad*, which set sail for a sugar plantation on the Island of Principe.

Desperate to escape, Cinque managed to pry a rusty nail out of the ship's side and use it to unfasten the chain that bound him and the other captives. The newly freed slaves then crept up on deck, where they killed the captain and most of the crew and captured Ruiz and Montes. Since the Africans knew nothing about sailing a ship that size, they were forced to rely on their two captives. Ordered to sail east for Africa, Montes tricked Cinque by changing direction at night so that the ship headed north.

Ruiz and Montes hoped to reach the southern United States, where slavery was legal. Instead, they landed north near Montauk Point on Long Island. When Cinque and some of the other Africans went ashore to find food and water, a U.S. Coast Guard ship appeared and forced the *Amistad* to surrender. Upon his return to the ship, Cinque was arrested. He and the others were charged with mutiny and murder.

The Spanish and Cuban authorities demanded that the United States return both the ship and the slaves to them. But U.S. abolitionists protested. Ruiz and Montes were the real criminals, they said, not Cinque and the other Africans.

Cinque's trial was held on January 7, 1840, in New Haven, Connecticut. It created a sensation. Classes at Yale Law School were dismissed so that students could attend the trial. Although Cinque and the others could not speak English, they argued through an interpreter that they had been kidnapped and had the right to resist by any means necessary. The court agreed, but the case was appealed. On September 17, 1840, the circuit court of appeals upheld the lower court's decision.

However, President Martin Van Buren, sympathetic to southern slaveholders, ordered the U.S. Justice Department to appeal the case once again—this time to the U.S. Supreme Court.

At this point, former President John Quincy Adams agreed to represent the Africans. Though he was then in his seventies and almost blind, Adams was still active in the antislavery movement. After an eight-and-a-half-hour argument before the court, Adams won the case. On March 9, 1841, Cinque and the others were ordered freed without delay. They returned to Africa, settling in Sierra Leone.

Mutinies on slave ships were not uncommon, due in part to the terrible treatment the slaves received. Chained together and packed into filthy ship holds under conditions so crowded that it was almost impossible to move, the slaves died by the thousands. Estimates of men, women, and children believed to have been imported from Africa to North and South America and the Caribbean range from 9,566,100 to 13,887,500 in the years between 1500 and 1870. In the late 1700s, when the trade was at its peak, an average of 80,000 people a year fell victim to the slave traders. Of these, 12.5 percent to 14.5 percent died before ever reaching the Americas. Some died from beatings; others committed suicide. But most succumbed to disease—dysentery, fever, and smallpox—brought on by the filthy, unsanitary conditions they were forced to endure.

In 1807 the U.S. government outlawed the importation of slaves. But enforcement was weak. The trade continued illegally, with thousands of Africans being smuggled in every year. It took the Civil War to end slavery in the United States and the African slave trade that went with it.

Slave mutiny aboard the *Amistad*

James Beckwourth

Frontiersman, Scout, Explorer
1798-1866

Trapper, trader, explorer, mountain man, army scout—James Beckwourth was all these things and so admired by the Crow Indians that they made him a chief.

Born in Fredericksburg, Virginia, to a black slave mother and a white father, James Beckwourth and his family later moved to Missouri. When he was nineteen, he was taken to St. Louis to learn a trade. But after getting into a fight with his master, Beckwourth took off for New Orleans. There he signed up as a scout for General William Henry Ashley's Rocky Mountain Fur Company.

Before long, he had become a famous mountain man, respected for his expert skill with a knife and a gun. In 1824 he was adopted by the Crow nation and married to a Crow woman. His remarkable courage earned him the name "Bloody Arm."

Beckwourth remained with the Indians for six years, then returned to St. Louis, where he joined the army. After serving as a scout during the Second (or Western) Seminole War, he traveled to California, where he prospected for gold. While working as chief scout for General John Frémont, Beckwourth discovered an important pass through the Sierra Nevada Mountains. The passage, now known as Beckwourth Pass, became an important route for wagon trains traveling west into California.

In 1866 the U.S. government asked Beckwourth to use his influence to establish peaceful relations with the Crow Indians. Happy to see him again, the Crow asked him to return to the tribe as a chief. Beckwourth, however, had other things in mind. The Indians prepared a farewell feast to honor him. However, when he sat down to enjoy the festivities, it turned out to be the last meal he ever ate. Legend has it that the Crow Indians poisoned him. Since they could not have him alive, they could at least keep his body and his powerful spirit with them. If the legend is true, the Crow no doubt meant to bestow a great honor on James Beckwourth—but one that he probably would have preferred to do without.

Madison Washington
Slave Insurrectionist

On the morning of October 27, 1841, the slave ship *Creole*, carrying 135 black slaves, set sail from Hampton Roads, Virginia, for New Orleans, Louisiana. Nine days later, the slaves, under the courageous leadership of Madison Washington, revolted.

This was not the first time Madison Washington had acted to obtain his freedom. A year earlier, he had escaped to Canada. However, he had been forced to leave behind his wife, Susan. A year later, carrying phony "free papers," he returned to Virginia to rescue her.

As an extra precaution, he had sewn miniature saws, files, and other tools into the lining of his clothes. Traveling mainly by night, he reached the plantation where his wife was a slave. Unfortunately, before he could reach her room, he was caught and placed aboard the *Creole* with other slaves who were to be sold in New Orleans.

Being an escaped slave, Washington was chained to the floor of the cabin where he could be watched closely. Since no one bothered to check his clothes, he was able to use his hidden tools to cut himself free. On the ninth day out, rough weather conditions kept the crew busy, giving Washington time to free other slaves.

That night, Washington, Ben Blacksmith, and seventeen other slaves secretly made their way to the quarterdeck where Captain Enson, first mate Mr. Merritt, and slave owner Henry Hewell were talking. On seeing the escaped slaves, Hewell quickly drew a pistol and killed one of them. Then Madison Washington killed Hewell.

The captain and the rest of the crew of the *Creole* were made prisoners and forced to sail the ship to a British colony. On November 9, 1841, the *Creole* dropped anchor at Nassau in the Bahamas. The slaves went ashore and asked for asylum.

The reaction in the United States was angry and swift. Supporters of slavery demanded that the British return the *Creole* and its slave cargo. They also insisted that the leaders of the revolt be tried for murder. Massachusetts Senator Charles Sumner, however, argued that Virginia's slave laws did not apply beyond the borders of the state.

Representative Joshua Giddings of Ohio praised the slaves for seeking their freedom. In fact, Giddings spoke so forcefully in favor of defying slavery that he was censured by the House of Representatives. He later resigned in protest but was promptly reelected.

Eventually, British authorities decided that the slaves from the *Creole* should remain free. Proslavery reaction in Congress was so strong, however, that the British agreed to pay an indemnity for failing to return the slave cargo.

Madison Washington not only had gained his freedom a second time but also was reunited with his wife, Susan. Although he had not known it, she was among the slaves aboard the *Creole*.

Norbert Rillieux

Inventor
1806-1894

On March 17, 1806, a child born in New Orleans, Louisiana, would one day make life a good deal sweeter for the entire sugar industry. His name was Norbert Rillieux, and he was the son of a hard-working plantation slave woman and a wealthy French engineer.

As a young man Rillieux was given his freedom and sent to Paris where he studied engineering at L'École Centrale. At age twenty-four, he became an instructor there, specializing in steam engine technology. He also developed a theory called "multiple-effect evaporation," which he applied to the process of sugar refining.

Previously, sugar had been obtained from sugarcane during a slow and expensive process called the "Jamaica Train." Groups of men (usually slaves) continually poured boiling sugarcane juice from one kettle to another until it was brown and lumpy. Rillieux designed a "multiple effect vacuum pan" evaporator that improved the quality of the sugar and produced it at a much lower cost. Soon, his machine was in great demand in the United States, Mexico, Cuba, and Caribbean countries.

Today, Norbert Rillieux's theories still form the basis for manufacturing sugar, soap, glue, gelatin, and condensed milk. Brilliant, hardworking, and proud, Norbert Rillieux took the bitter with the sweet and, in the words of Charles Browne, a U.S. Department of Agriculture chemist, produced "[an] invention [that] is the greatest in the history of American chemical engineering. . . ."

The Underground Railroad

It was called the Underground Railroad, but it didn't run on tracks. It was a secret escape system for runaway slaves. Those using it needed courage and determination—not tickets. The runaways traveled through fields and swamps, woods and back country roads; across rivers, creeks, and mountains; by boat, wagon, horse, train, and on foot. Sometimes they headed north toward Canada, sometimes west toward Mexico, and sometimes south toward Spanish-owned Florida, the Bahamas, and the free islands of the Caribbean. Yet, no matter in which direction these men and women headed, their destination was always the same—freedom.

The first twenty black indentured servants arrived in Jamestown, Virginia, around the end of August 1619. By 1641 Massachusetts had legalized slavery, and other colonies soon followed.

From the beginning, there was resistance to slavery—resistance that grew stronger with the signing of the Declaration of Independence proclaiming freedom as an inalienable right. In 1777 Vermont became the first colony to abolish slavery. The next year, the Continental Congress forbade slavery in the Northwest Territory. By 1804 slavery had been outlawed either partially or completely in the states of Massachusetts, New Hampshire, Rhode Island, Pennsylvania, Connecticut, and New Jersey.

Although the slave system remained strong throughout the South, pressure against it continued, forcing Congress to forbid the importation of new slaves into the United States after January 1, 1808. Twelve years later, in 1820, the Missouri Compromise outlawed slavery north of 36° 30′ north latitude (with the exception of Missouri).

The pressure to end slavery came from abolitionists—whites and free blacks who wanted to see slavery abolished. Within this group were individuals such as Benjamin Franklin, Thomas Paine, and the Marquis de Lafayette. Abolitionists such as these made hundreds of speeches, organized dozens of antislavery meetings, and repeatedly petitioned the president and other political leaders to end slavery.

Those people willing to help slaves escape became agents of the Underground Railroad and included human rights leaders Frederick Douglass, Harriet Tubman, Sojourner Truth, William Lloyd Garrison, Susan B. Anthony, Congressman Thaddeus Stevens, famous detective Allen Pinkerton, writers Henry David Thoreau and Harriet Beecher Stowe, and poet John Greenleaf Whittier.

Some of these people, such as Harriet Tubman, acted as "conductors," slipping deep into slave territory to meet with runaways and guide them to safety. Others, such as Frederick Douglass, operated "stations" or "depots"—safe places where runaways could hide as they made their way to freedom. Jermain Loguen, once a slave himself, helped more than 1,500 to escape, and Levi Coffin, a Quaker who was called the "President of the Underground Railroad," helped more than 3,000 to escape.

Slaves also found safety and support among American Indians, such as the Ottawa of Ohio, the Shinnecock of New England, and the Seminole of Florida.

Still, all of this help from free blacks and antislavery whites would have done little good had it not been for the actions of the slaves themselves. Although slaveholders insisted that their slaves were happy and contented, it was clear that the opposite was true. Forced to work long hours in the hot sun, many slaves suffered punishments. Families were torn apart as husbands and wives were separated and children sold. Even slaves who were well-treated resented their situation and wished to be free.

No one knows for sure how many slaves fled—100,000, 200,000, maybe more—or what their escapes involved. We know that one man hid in a crate and had himself mailed north. Another carved a pair of wooden shoes that he wore as he walked more than 1,500 miles to freedom.

All slaves used song lyrics to pass on secret information and provide instructions for successful escape. For example, the old spiritual "Wade in the Water," meant to wade in the waters of rivers and streams so that dogs could not pick up your scent. The hymn "Follow the Risen Lord" was turned into "Follow the Drinking Gourd." The drinking gourd referred to the Little Dipper, the constellation in the sky that included the North Star, a guide to the north. And "Swing Low, Sweet Chariot, Coming for to Carry Me Home" meant that a conductor on the Underground Railroad was coming to "carry" you "home" to freedom.

Slave owners hired slave hunters to track down and recapture escaped slaves, and they offered money for information leading to the whereabouts of people like Harriet Tubman. In return for allowing California to enter the Union as a free state, slaveholders insisted that Congress pass the Fugitive Slave Law, which required citizens to help law officers apprehend and return escaped slaves.

Many Underground Railroad activists were sent to prison. Others, like newspaper editor Elijah Lovejoy, were murdered. But slaves continued to run away, and the Underground Railroad continued to function, until the Civil War finally ran slavery off the track.

Lewis Temple

Inventor
1800-1854

In 1848 Lewis Temple invented a new kind of harpoon and, with it, hooked the entire American whaling industry.

Born in Richmond, Virginia, in 1800, Lewis Temple later made his way to New Bedford, Massachusetts. Although very little is known about his early life, it is possible that he was an escaped slave. New Bedford was an important stop, or "station," on the Underground Railroad, and many runaway slaves passed through there.

After settling in New Bedford in 1839, Temple opened up a blacksmith shop and married Mary Clark. By 1836 he was making harpoons, lances, and other equipment used on whaling ships.

After hearing sailors complain that whales frequently pulled loose from their harpoons and escaped, Temple designed a new type that would hold them securely. His harpoon had a movable head or "toggle." Once it entered the whale, it would not come loose. Far superior to the ordinary barbed-head harpoon, "Temple's Toggle," as it was called, was an immediate success. In 1845 he was able to construct a larger shop.

Unfortunately, a few years later, Lewis Temple was badly injured in a fall. Unable to work, he sued the city of New Bedford for $2,000. A few months later, in May 1854, he died.

Lewis Temple's wife sold his shop to pay their debts, and there was little left. But whalers were left with plenty. They had Temple's Toggle, the invention that revolutionized the whaling industry.

Dred Scott

Slave
1795-1858

In 1846 a slave named Dred Scott sued his owners for his freedom. After several trials and appeals, the case reached the U.S. Supreme Court. The final decision made history and brought the United States one step closer to the Civil War.

Dred Scott was born a slave in Southampton County, Virginia, around 1795. After the death of his owner, Peter Blow, in 1831, he was sold to John Emerson, a U.S. Army surgeon stationed in Missouri, a slave state.

In the course of his army service, Dr. Emerson was transferred to Fort Armstrong in Rock Island, Illinois. (Illinois was a free state, and slavery was prohibited there.) Dr. Emerson, considering himself still a resident of Missouri and living only temporarily in Illinois, believed that it was legal to have his slave, Dred Scott, with him. Two years later, Dr. Emerson was transferred to the free territory of Wisconsin. Once again, Dred Scott accompanied him and his wife. Then in 1839, they all returned to Missouri.

When Dr. Emerson died in 1843, Scott tried to purchase freedom for himself and his family. When Mrs. Emerson refused his request, he sued. He argued that because he had lived for several years in free territory, he should be free.

Scott lost his initial court battle but sued again—this time winning in a St. Louis court in 1850. This ruling, however, was overturned by the Missouri Supreme Court in 1852. With the aid of white abolitionist supporters and friends, Dred Scott decided to appeal his case to the U.S. Supreme Court. He had little chance of winning his case, however. The chief justice, Roger B. Taney, was a southerner who favored slavery.

On March 6, 1857, the U.S. Supreme Court handed down its decision: as a black man, Dred Scott was not a citizen of the United States and had no right to sue anybody. Furthermore, the court ruled that Congress could not prevent slave owners from taking their property (in this case, slaves) anywhere in the country. This meant that all anti-slavery laws, including the Missouri Compromise that outlawed slavery north of 36° 30′ north latitude, were unconstitutional. In the words of Chief Justice Taney, blacks were an "inferior class of beings" who "had no rights which the white man was bound to respect."

The reaction to the U.S. Supreme Court ruling was immediate and widespread. Mass meetings were held throughout the North and West, protesting the decision. Many blacks and whites gave up hope of ever ending slavery. But Frederick Douglass, the famous abolitionist, was not discouraged. "The Supreme Court is not the only power in this world," he said. "Judge Taney cannot bail out the ocean . . . or pluck the silvery star of liberty from our Northern sky."

As for Dred Scott, he remained in Missouri, where he died two years later. Although he had not gained his freedom, his lawsuit led to a court decision that helped bring about the Civil War by ending any hope for a peaceful solution to slavery.

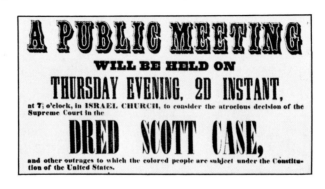

A PUBLIC MEETING WILL BE HELD ON THURSDAY EVENING, 2D INSTANT, at 7½ o'clock, in ISRAEL CHURCH, to consider the atrocious decision of the Supreme Court in the DRED SCOTT CASE, and other outrages to which the colored people are subject under the Constitution of the United States.

Lewis Hayden

Abolitionist, State Legislator
1815-1889

His mother was so badly treated that she became insane and attempted suicide. His brothers and sisters were all sold at an auction, and Lewis Hayden himself was traded for a pair of carriage horses. When he finally escaped, he spent his life trying to free others.

Married while still in his teens, Hayden and his fourteen-year-old wife eventually had three children. But one died and another was sold "nobody knows where." Although he had several opportunities to run away, to do so would have meant leaving his family behind; so Lewis Hayden waited.

Finally, when his son was ten years old, Hayden and his family escaped with the help of two white abolitionist teachers, Calvin Fairbank and Delia Webster. The Haydens made their way safely from Lexington, Kentucky, to Ohio and then to Canada. But Fairbank and Webster were arrested and charged with slave stealing. In February 1845, Fairbank agreed to plead guilty if Webster were allowed to go free. As a result, Webster was freed, and Fairbank was sentenced to fifteen years in prison.

Meanwhile, Lewis Hayden and his family moved to Detroit, Michigan, where he established a school for black children. Hearing of Fairbank's imprisonment, Hayden raised $650 and sent it to his old owner. In return, his owner agreed to petition the governor of Kentucky to free Fairbank. On August 23, 1849, Fairbank was released after spending four years in prison.

Hayden then moved his family to Boston, where he became active in the Underground Railroad. His house served as the main Boston station, sheltering hundreds of runaway slaves.

Among these runaways were William and Ellen Craft. On the day their owner sent slave catchers to arrest them, Hayden barricaded his house and threatened to blow it up if a slave hunter set foot inside. Meanwhile, the Crafts escaped to safety, and the slave catchers were forced to return home without an arrest.

The following year, Lewis Hayden was arrested for helping a slave named Shadrach escape. Although he was brought to trial, Hayden was acquitted after the jury, in spite of the strong evidence, refused to convict him.

In 1854 Hayden, Reverend Thomas Wentworth Higginson, and a group of fifteen white men and ten black men tried to free a runaway slave named Anthony Burns who was being held in a Boston jail. The men broke down the courthouse door and a wild fight took place. But they were forced out of the building, and shortly afterwards, Burns was returned south to slavery.

When the Civil War broke out, Hayden helped recruit blacks for the Union army. His own son enlisted in the navy and was killed in action.

Lewis Hayden spent his later years working for civil rights for blacks and for women. He was elected to the Massachusetts legislature and arranged for a monument to be erected to the memory of the black revolutionary war hero Crispus Attucks.

Although there is no monument to Lewis Hayden, he—like Crispus Attucks, whom he admired—was a true American hero.

Harriet Tubman

Abolitionist
1821-1913

"On my underground railroad I never ran my train off the track. And I never lost a passenger."—Harriet Tubman

WANTED DEAD OR ALIVE—$40,000 REWARD! That was the price slaveholders were willing to pay for Harriet Tubman, a small black woman who ran away from slavery in 1849 and spent the next sixteen years of her life trying to free others.

Born in Dorchester County, Maryland, around 1821, Harriet Tubman was one of eleven children. Although highly intelligent, she was not allowed to attend school or learn to read or write. Instead, she spent her childhood working in the fields. At age fifteen or sixteen, her master threw a rock at her when she tried to protect another slave from an angry overseer. The blow almost killed her, and for the rest of her life she suffered from seizures that caused her to "black out" briefly. She also began to see visions and hear voices warning her of danger and urging her to make her way north to freedom.

When she was twenty-eight years old, she did just that. Guided by the North Star, she made her way to Philadelphia. But personal freedom was not enough for Harriet Tubman. She joined the Underground Railroad and made approximately nineteen dangerous trips to the South to bring more than 300 slaves (including her aged parents) to freedom.

She earned money for her rescue mission by working as a cook and a laundress. When she had saved enough money, she would disguise herself and make her way south into slave territory. White people who happened to run into her saw only a harmless, half-crazy old woman, wandering along singing religious songs. What they did not know was that the songs were a code alerting slaves to her arrival.

Harriet Tubman's rules of escape were very simple: be on time; tell no one of your plans; follow commands without complaint; and, most important, be prepared to die rather than turn back. She meant what she said. Tubman often carried a gun and threatened to shoot anyone who tried to quit. No one ever did.

Harriet Tubman planned her escapes for Saturday nights. That gave her groups at least a thirty-six-hour head start before angry slave owners could get their wanted posters out on Monday. Harriet never lost a passenger on her Underground Railroad.

During the Civil War, she worked as a scout, a spy, and a nurse for the Union army. She is known to have led a raid that resulted in the freedom of over 750 slaves. Following the war, she attempted to establish schools for black people and later worked in support of women's rights.

Harriet Tubman lived to be ninety-two. When she died, she was buried in Ohio with military honors. Flags flew at half-mast in New York as whites and blacks gathered to pay tribute to the woman they called "the general" and the "Moses of Her People."

In 1978 the U.S. Postal Service issued a Harriet Tubman stamp in honor of the small black woman who, through her courage and determination, had placed her own stamp on American history.

Jermain Wesley Loguen

Abolitionist
1813-1872

Harriet Tubman helped 300 people escape from slavery, but she needed the help of Jermain Wesley Loguen, a dedicated abolitionist, to gain her own freedom.

Jermain Loguen was born near Nashville, Tennessee. His mother, a free black woman, had been kidnapped and sold to David Logue. Although Logue became Jermain's father, he cared nothing about the boy or his mother and sold them both. The suffering his mother had to endure, the sale of his sister, and the brutal murder of another slave convinced Jermain to run away.

He was twenty-one when he escaped north to Detroit, Michigan, and then to Canada, where he went to school. Returning to the United States, he continued his education at the Oneida Institute in New York. Later, he opened two schools for black children in New York. In 1842 he became an ordained Methodist minister and established the Abolition Church and five smaller churches. Sometime during this period he changed the name his father had given him, Jarm Logue, to Jermain Loguen.

Jermain Loguen strongly supported the movement to end slavery. He worked closely with Frederick Douglass and often wrote articles for Douglass's *North Star* newspaper. Loguen was also an important conductor on the Underground Railroad. Harriet Tubman was just one of approximately 1,500 runaway slaves he helped to escape.

After the end of the Civil War and the passage of the Thirteenth

Amendment to the Constitution, which ended slavery, Jermain Loguen became more active in the African Methodist Episcopal Zion Church. Yet, it is for his work as an abolitionist and conductor on the Underground Railroad that he is remembered. At a time when such activities could have led to his imprisonment, reenslavement, and even death, Jermain Wesley Loguen stood fast and helped 1,500 runaways ride the Underground Railroad's "Freedom Train."

A station on the Underground Railroad in Andover, Massachusetts

John Anthony Copeland, Jr.

Abolitionist
1836-1859

"I am not terrified by the gallows . . .upon which I am soon to stand and suffer death for doing what George Washington was made a hero for doing." John Anthony Copeland, a black revolutionary soon to be hanged along with John Brown for his part in the attack on Harpers Ferry, wrote these words in a letter to his family.

Born free in 1836 in Raleigh, North Carolina, John Copeland grew up in Ohio. There he had been thrown in jail for helping free John Price, a runaway slave who was about to be returned to his owner. Shortly after being released from prison, he and his uncle, Lewis Leary, joined the famous white abolitionist, John Brown.

Brown intended to seize the federal arsenal located at Harpers Ferry, West Virginia, and lead a revolt against slaveholders that would bring an end to slavery.

On the night of October 16, 1859, John Brown, together with twenty-one followers, including his own two sons, began their raid. Besides John Copeland and Lewis Leary, there were three other black men: Shields Green, a runaway slave; Dangerfield Newby, a free black hoping to free his slave wife and children; and a college student named Osborne Perry Anderson.

Silently, the men crossed the river to Harpers Ferry, captured the armory guards, and took control of the arsenal. But the alarm had been sounded, bringing Virginia militiamen to the engine house where the raiders were holed up. Toward evening, a trainload of U.S. marines, led by Colonel Robert E. Lee, arrived to apprehend them.

Dangerfield Newby was the first to die, followed by John Brown's two sons, Lewis Leary, and six others. John Copeland, Shields Green, John Brown, and four others were captured. Osborne Anderson escaped.

After a lengthy trial, John Brown and the others were found guilty of treason and murder and sentenced to death. John Copeland was hanged alongside Shields Green on December 16, 1859. His last words were "I am dying for freedom. I could not die for a better cause."

Drawing of John Brown on his way to his execution

Frederick Douglass

Abolitionist, Orator
1817-1895

"Save the Negro and you save the nation. Destroy the Negro and you destroy the nation, and to save both you must have but one great law of Liberty, Equality and Fraternity for all Americans . . . ."
— Frederick Douglass

Frederick Augustus Washington Bailey (Frederick Douglass) didn't know the exact date of his birth. He picked February 14 for his birthday because his mother used to call him her "little valentine."

Born a slave on a Maryland plantation, Frederick never knew for sure who his father was. When he was still a baby, his mother was sent to work on a plantation miles away. Sometimes, after work, she would walk twelve miles back to see him before he went to sleep. But in the morning, she would be gone. When Douglass was about seven, she died.

Often, Douglass was so hungry that he would fight with the dog, "Old Nep," for bits of food that had been thrown out. Even worse was the cold. He, like other slave children, wore only a long, rough, knee-length shirt—no shoes, no jacket, no pants. In winter, he would take an old sack and wrap himself in it. It was his only blanket as he slept on the floor at night.

Master Anthony's daughter, Lucretia Auld, took a liking to Frederick. At her suggestion, he was sent to Baltimore as a companion to her nephew, Tommy Auld. There Frederick learned to read and write.

When Frederick Douglass was sixteen, Lucretia Auld died and he was ordered back to the plantation. One day, after refusing to obey his master, Douglass was hired out to Mr. Covey, a well-known slave breaker. Intending to force Douglass into submission, Covey beat him regularly, denied him food, and forced him to labor in the fields twelve to fourteen hours a day. Douglass fought back.

Later, he was hired out to another farmer who treated him more kindly. But whether he was treated well or badly, Douglass dreamed constantly of being free. Together with five other men, he made plans to steal a boat, row seventy miles to the Chesapeake Bay, and from there hike north into Pennsylvania. Able to write, Douglass forged passes. But before their plans could be carried out, they were arrested and thrown in jail. Douglass was sent back to Baltimore, where he was hired out to work in the shipyards. There, he met and fell in love with Anna Murray, a freeborn black woman. Together they plotted his second escape attempt.

On September 3, 1838, using the borrowed indentification papers of a friendly black sailor, and taking with him a small amount of money that Anna had been able to save from nine years of work, Douglass escaped to New York. Once there, he went to the home of David Ruggles, a black abolitionist. Ruggles took him in and helped make arrangements for Anna to come to New York. As soon as Anna arrived, she and Frederick were married. The next day, they boarded a steamer for New Bedford, Massachusetts.

In New Bedford, to avoid slave hunters, Douglass changed his last name from Bailey to Douglass. While there, he met William Lloyd Garrison, publisher of an antislavery newspaper, *The Liberator.* He also began speaking to audiences about his life as a slave.

Soon, the Massachusetts Antislavery Society asked Douglass to speak on their behalf. He spoke so fluently that many of his listeners began to doubt that he had ever been a slave. To convince them, he wrote *Narrative of the Life of Frederick Douglass, An American*

Slave. Information in the book regarding slaves, owners, and places was so specific that he became worried his old owner would read of his whereabouts, so he traveled to England.

There he continued to lecture against slavery. He also spoke out in favor of Irish freedom, women's rights, and world peace. His keen intelligence, brilliant speaking ability, and impressive appearance won him numerous friends. They encouraged him to remain in England. But he felt that to do so would be to abandon black Americans still trapped by slavery. Douglass was still a fugitive, however, and even more famous now than when he had left the United States. Since his return would be dangerous, a group of English supporters arranged to purchase his freedom so that he could return home safely.

When Douglass returned to the United States in 1847, he settled in Rochester, New York, where he established a newspaper called *North Star.* The name was chosen because runaway slaves heading north without compasses often used the North Star in the Little Dipper constellation as their guide.

Title page of Frederick Douglass's book, published by the Antislavery Office in 1846

NARRATIVE

OF THE

LIFE

OF

FREDERICK DOUGLASS,

AN

AMERICAN SLAVE.

WRITTEN BY HIMSELF.

BOSTON:
PUBLISHED AT THE ANTI-SLAVERY OFFICE,
No. 25 CORNHILL.
1846.

The paper's motto, "Right is of no sex—Truth is of no color—God is the Father of us all, and all we are brethren," set the tone for Douglass's writing. Although he was concerned mainly with the abolition of slavery, he also favored equal rights for women and Indians, supported public education, and wanted to end the death penalty.

In 1848 Douglass met with John Brown, who later led the famous raid on Harpers Ferry. After the raid, the governor of Virginia, thinking that Douglass was conspiring with Brown, put out a warrant for Douglass's arrest. To escape imprisonment, he fled to Canada and remained there until 1860.

Douglass returned to the United States shortly after the Civil War began. He encouraged President Lincoln to free all the slaves immediately and allow them to enlist in the Union forces. After Lincoln issued the Emancipation Proclamation, freeing slaves in Confederate-held territory and allowing blacks to enlist, Douglass recruited men for the Fifty-fourth and Fifty-fifth Massachusetts regiments. Among the first to enlist were his own two sons.

Over the next fourteen years, Douglass had several presidential posts: marshall of the District of Columbia, recorder of deeds, and minister-resident and consul-general to Haiti and the Dominican Republic.

After retiring from public office, Douglass focused on the mounting problems of segregation and lynching. Outraged by the situation, he joined the antilynching crusade of Mary Church Terrell and Ida Wells-Barnett. But this battle was to be left to others. On February 20, 1895, Frederick Douglass died of a heart attack.

Often considered the foremost black leader of the nineteenth century, Douglass also has been referred to as the father of the civil rights movement. Outstanding speaker, writer, political analyst, and diplomat, Frederick Douglass saw, as many others did not, that the dream of American democracy could never be fulfilled as long as slavery and injustice prevailed.

Sojourner Truth

Abolitionist, Women's Rights Activist, Preacher
1797-1883

"I have borne thirteen children and seen them almost all sold off into slavery, and when I cried out with my mother's grief none but Jesus Heard." — Sojourner Truth

They called her a "Pilgrim of God" because she said the Lord had sent her to travel the countryside and to "declare the truth unto people." Born in 1797, in Hurley, New York, Sojourner Truth (or Isabella Baumfree, as she was named originally) sought in religion a sanctuary from the terrible cruelties she suffered as a slave. Sold four times, she ran away in 1826, one year before slavery was officially ended in New York. With the help of a Quaker family, she won a lawsuit to have her son returned to her (he had been sold at age five to a slave owner in Alabama).

For the next few years, Sojourner Truth worked in New York and attended various churches, hoping to satisfy her religious yearnings. Then in 1843, she said a voice from God told her to leave the city and to take the name "Sojourner." The voice told her "to travel up and down the land showing the people their sins and being a sign unto them." When Sojourner asked the Lord for a second name, she said he gave her the name "Truth" because she was to tell everyone the truth about slavery.

For nearly twenty years she traveled across the country speaking out on slavery and women's rights. Though not an eloquent speaker, she was dramatic and very effective. Her statements on slavery won her the respect of Frederick Douglass, William Lloyd Garrison, and other well-known abolitionists, and she was invited to meet with Abraham Lincoln at the White House.

When the Civil War began, Sojourner Truth raised money for black Union soldiers by lecturing and singing. In 1862 she moved to Arlington, Virginia, near Washington, D.C., to help newly freed slaves adjust to freedom. It was there that she became the first "Freedom Rider."

Until 1865, horse cars in Washington were segregated. When Congress outlawed segregation, Sojourner Truth decided to make sure the new law was obeyed. One day, after several horse cars refused to stop for her, she stood in the middle of the road, waving her arms and shouting: "I want to ride! I want to ride!" Before long, a crowd gathered and forced the next horse car to stop. Truth climbed aboard and refused to move when the conductor tried to throw her off. Unable to budge her, the conductor gave in. But Sojourner Truth was not quite through making her point. To make sure everyone was aware of the new law, she had the conductor arrested and then fired from his job.

Sojourner Truth spent the remainder of her life trying to obtain land out West for newly freed slaves. She died on November 23, 1883.

George Washington

Pioneer, City Founder
1817-1905

On August 15, 1817, a son was born to a black male slave and a free white woman near Winchester in Frederick County, Virginia. The boy was given the name George Washington. One day, he would establish the city of Centralia, Washington. At the time of his birth, however, life did not look as promising for him on the east side of the country.

George's father was sold shortly after he was born, and his mother gave the baby to a white couple, James and Anna Cochran, to raise. A few years later, the Cochrans moved to Missouri with George.

Although he never attended school, young George taught himself to read and do arithmetic. He also learned to tan leather, sew clothes, and cook. When he grew up, he began operating a sawmill in St. Joseph. Things were going well until a white man refused to pay him for a load of lumber. Washington took the man to court, but the case was thrown out. The judge told him that blacks didn't have the right to sue.

Frustrated with the laws in Missouri, Washington and his foster parents moved to Illinois. There they were required to post a bond guaranteeing their good behavior.

At the time, Illinois and Missouri were not the only states to limit black rights. Several states denied blacks the right to vote. Others required them to pay special taxes and forbade them to testify in court against whites.

Since Washington didn't have the money to post a bond, he and his foster parents moved again—this time to Oregon Territory. There he staked out a 640-acre plot. But he soon learned that Oregon Territory prohibited black property ownership. This time, however, Washington got around the law by putting his land in his foster parents' name.

In 1853 a section of the Oregon Territory broke away to form what is now Washington State. George Washington's land was within this section. The creation of the new territory did not affect his plans until 1872, when the Northern Pacific Railroad laid track across the land. Washington saw this as a wonderful opportunity to establish a town. He called it Centerville because it was located midway between Kalama and Tacoma (the cities that the railroad connected). Later, the name was changed to Centralia.

In 1875 Washington began selling town lots for $10 apiece to anyone willing to build on them. He also donated property for the First Baptist Church and cemetery and, in 1881, provided land for a public square.

Centralia was hit by a serious economic depression in 1893, largely because of the rerouting of the railroad. Although hundreds of people were forced to leave the new town, Washington refused to let it die. He gave away clothing and tons of food to those who chose to stay. He lent money to some people so they could pay their bills, and he hired others to work for him so they could get by.

In 1905, at the age of eighty-eight, Washington suffered severe injuries in a buggy accident. Shortly afterward, he died. On the day of his funeral—the largest ever seen in the city—all businesses closed. Memorial services were held in the church that he had established. George Washington was buried in the cemetery he had donated to Centralia, the city he had not only founded but also saved.

Robert Smalls

Civil War Hero, Congressman
1839-1915

One of the most famous heroes of the Civil War was a twenty-three-year-old man named Robert Smalls. When the war started, Robert Smalls was assigned to the slave crew of a Confederate dispatch ship called the *Planter*. On the night of May 13, 1862, the *Planter* lay anchored in the harbor at Charleston, South Carolina. Her captain, a man named Relyea, and other officers had gone ashore after spending the day hauling guns.

It was then that Robert Smalls decided to make his move. An expert sailor, he knew the tides, shoals, and currents and could handle the ship easily. After first smuggling aboard his wife, children, and five other people, he and the eight-man crew hoisted anchor and maneuvered the *Planter* out into the main channel.

The risks were great. Fort Sumter, well-armed and in Confederate hands, overlooked Charleston harbor. Morris Island, also well-armed and under Confederate control, stood between Robert Smalls and the Union navy. Even if he succeeded in getting past these two strongholds without being stopped, there was always the chance the Union ships would fire on the *Planter*, not realizing it was no longer under enemy control. But Smalls, believing in the importance of the escape, was ready to take the risk.

The Confederate soldiers guarding Fort Sumter watched the *Planter* glide past. Robert Smalls, wearing the captain's large straw hat, stood on deck with his arms folded. The soldiers, thinking they recognized Captain Relyea, were not suspicious at first. When they finally realized their mistake, it was too late. They tried to signal Morris Island, but the *Planter* was already in open water, out of range of Confederate guns.

When Smalls reached Union territory, he turned the *Planter* over to the Yankee fleet and then joined the Union forces. Everyone was amazed at his courage and boldness. One slave was overheard saying to another, "Robert Smalls, Robert Smalls, that's all you ever talk about. Robert Smalls ain't God, you know." "Yeah, I know," said his friend, "but don't forget, Smalls is young yet."

Congress awarded Robert Smalls and the rest of the crew one-half the appraised value of the *Planter* (Smalls received $1,500). He was made a captain in the Union navy and given command of the *Planter* until the end of the war. Afterward, he returned to South Carolina, where he was elected first to the South Carolina House of Representatives and then to the state senate. Later, he served in the U.S. Congress.

While in office, Smalls worked to secure laws that promoted black education and provided increased financial opportunities for them. Even though slavery had ended, many former slave owners were attempting to restrict black progress, first through the courts and state legislatures, and, when that didn't work, through threats and violence.

Robert Smalls, however, was never intimidated. In 1913, at the age of seventy-four, he single-handedly saved two black men from being lynched. Two years later, Robert Smalls, Civil War hero and fighter for civil rights, died in Beaufort, South Carolina.

Charlotte Forten Grimke

Educator, Writer, Abolitionist
1837-1914

"Let us labor to acquire knowledge, to break down the barriers of prejudice and oppression... believing that if not for us, for another generation there is a brighter day in store...." — Charlotte Forten

On a cool fall day in October 1862, a ship pulled away from the dock in New York City. On board was a frail, twenty-seven-year-old woman on her way to a new life on the Sea Islands off the coast of South Carolina.

Charlotte Forten, a free black from a wealthy family in Philadelphia, was a teacher. Although free and well-educated, she understood only too well the humiliation and pain of racial prejudice.

As a child, she had been denied admittance to Philadelphia schools because of her color. For the next few years, she was tutored at home. Then, at age sixteen, she was sent to live with the Charles Remond family in Salem, Massachusetts, so she could attend the integrated schools there. Like her own parents, the Remonds were active abolitionists. Their home had become the headquarters for antislavery lecturers passing through the city. Charlotte often met the great speakers of the antislavery movement: William Lloyd Garrison, Wendell Phillips, John Greenleaf Whittier, and William Wells Brown.

Racial discrimination had a profound effect upon Charlotte. Just how strongly it shaped her thoughts is revealed in a journal that she began when she was seventeen.

"I wonder that every colored person is not a misanthrope [hater of people]. Surely we have something to make us hate mankind. I have met girls in the schoolroom. They have been thoroughly kind and cordial to me. Perhaps the next day I have met them in the street. They feared to recognize me. . . . These are but trifles, certainly, to the great, public wrongs that we as a people are obliged to endure. But to those who experience them, these apparent trifles are most wearing and discouraging."[3]

In 1856 Charlotte Forten graduated from Salem Normal School with honors and began teaching. She also read constantly, often completing as many as 100 books a year. And she continued to support the abolitionist movement. In March 1858, illness forced her to resign her job and return to Philadelphia. But three years later, with the outbreak of the Civil War, Charlotte Forten saw a chance to serve her people.

Union forces had captured Hilton Head and the Sea Islands off the coast of South Carolina. Hundreds of slaves had taken advantage of the situation to flee to Union lines. Thousands of others were freed by advancing U.S. troops. Faced with huge numbers of largely illiterate, destitute ex-slaves, the government decided to recruit a group of young men and women to teach them. Charlotte Forten gladly volunteered.

Life in the Sea Islands was hard. Charlotte was not accustomed to the heat. Although her students were black, their ways were very different from what she had known. Even their language was different — a mixture of English and African words that had become a unique dialect over the years.

Along with reading and writing, she attempted to show her new students what black people could accomplish. In her journal entry dated Nov. 13, she writes: ". . . Talked to the children a little while today about the noble Toussaint (Toussaint L'Ouverture, who freed the slaves in Haiti). They listened very attentively. It is well that they should know what one of their own color could do for his race. I long to inspire them with courage and ambition . . . and high purpose."

When Charlotte Forten returned home to Philadelphia in May 1864, it was with a feeling of success. Two thousand children were enrolled in schools on the Sea Islands, and thousands of adults were learning to read.

For the next several years, she taught occasionally and gained a reputation as a writer. In 1878 she married the Reverend Francis J. Grimke, a man whose sermons reflected her own views of racial equality.

Charlotte Forten Grimke died on July 23, 1914, after a lingering illness. Not only had she shown by her life that education is the key to opportunity, but she also helped others to realize it. Her journal and writings reveal her as a sensitive yet courageous woman, unyielding in the face of racial prejudice and determined to help those less fortunate than herself.

The Emancipation Proclamation

I n 1858 Abraham Lincoln ran for senator of Illinois on the Republican ticket against Democrat Stephen A. Douglas. At that time, Lincoln said, "A house divided against itself cannot stand. I believe this government cannot endure permanently half slave and half free."

Although Lincoln lost the election, his opposition to slavery was reported widely. When he ran for president in 1860, southern democrats threatened to secede (withdraw) from the Union if he won. He did win, and six weeks later South Carolina voted to leave the Union. Mississippi, Florida, Alabama, Georgia, Louisiana, and Texas followed. By February 1861, they formed the Confederate States of America with Jefferson Davis as president.

Two months later, on April 12, 1861, Confederate forces attacked Fort Sumter in South Carolina, and the Civil War began. Four more slave states—Virginia, North Carolina, Arkansas, and Tennessee—joined the Confederacy. The remaining slave states—Maryland, Delaware, Kentucky, and Missouri (also known as the border states)—did not. To keep their allegiance, Lincoln moved cautiously on the issue of freeing slaves. At first, he recommended that slave owners receive payment for freed slaves. To calm white fears, he did not allow blacks to serve in the army. But as the fighting dragged on, white attitudes began to change.

On January 1, 1863, Abraham Lincoln issued the Emancipation Proclamation. The document stated that slaves in Confederate-held territory (about three-fourths of all slaves) should be considered free, and blacks could enlist in the Union forces.*

Many slaves, encouraged by the proclamation, tried to escape to Union lines. Others revolted. In the North, more than thirty black regiments had begun training for the war; several had already seen combat. By the end of the year, over 50,000 black soldiers were serving in the Union army.

*See pages 220-221 for the Emancipation Proclamation.

The Emancipation Proclamation, however, did not apply to the 800,000 slaves in the four border states that had not seceded or to those in territory under Union control. But the proclamation had its effect in these areas just the same. Army recruiters, promising freedom, encouraged thousands of slaves to run away and enlist. This, together with growing antislavery sentiments, greatly undermined the whole institution of slavery in these areas.

Of course, issuing the Emancipation Proclamation and enforcing it were two different things. Slavery in Confederate controlled territory continued to exist until the territory came under Union control. Still, the proclamation gave hope to thousands of blacks and whites who had fought to outlaw slavery. Allowing black soldiers to enlist helped turn the tide against the South. More importantly, the proclamation firmly placed the president and the federal government in a position to support freedom for all, regardless of race.

Black Civil War Soldiers

When the Civil War began, thousands of black Americans tried to enlist in the Union army. Jacob Dodson, a black frontiersman who had served with Kit Carson and General John Frémont, offered to raise a force of 300 black men to defend Washington, D.C. And Dr. G. P. Miller of Michigan wrote the secretary of war, offering to raise an army of up to 10,000 freemen. Both were turned down.

Although President Lincoln personally opposed slavery, he was concerned that if slavery were made the main issue of the war, the four slave states still in the Union—Delaware, Maryland, Kentucky, and Missouri—would secede. Also, he feared many Northerners would not support a war to free blacks. Frederick Douglass protested bitterly, calling this policy "weak and contemptible tenderness toward bloodthirsty slaveholding traitors . . . ." But he could not convince Lincoln. In fact, in the early days of the war, Union troops were instructed to return runaway slaves to their owners.

Many white soldiers refused to accept the official slave policy. General David Hunter, fighting in South Carolina, tried to arm several thousand former slaves but was stopped. General Ben Butler of Virginia was more successful. He declared captured or escaped slaves as "contraband" (illegal goods) and ordered them freed. Within two months, 900 "contrabands" were working for the Union army.

Often, slaves helped white Union soldiers who were trapped in Confederate territory. In the words of one Union soldier, "To see a black face was to find a true heart." Many other slaves risked their lives to provide Union commanders with information about Confederate plans and operations.

As Union soldiers continued to die, pressure to allow blacks to serve began to build. Secretary of the Navy Gideon Welles made the first move on September 25, 1861. He authorized the enlistment of black sailors at $10 a month and one meal a day. A little more than a year later, the Emancipation Proclamation allowed blacks to enlist in the Union army. By that time black military units already were fighting in

Louisiana, Missouri, and South Carolina.

Within seven months of the signing of the proclamation, more than thirty black regiments were in existence. By 1865 there were 166 all-black regiments. In all, approximately 180,000 black soldiers and 29,511 black sailors (one out of every four, most of them former slaves) fought for the Union. Another 200,000 men and women served as scouts, spies, laborers, blacksmiths, nurses, cooks, and guides.

Yet, black soldiers were not treated well. They were forced to serve in segregated units, almost always under the command of white officers. Often, they received inferior equipment and lacked medical supplies. Near the end of the war, they were still being paid only $10 a month (usually, $3 was withheld to pay for uniforms and equipment) while white soldiers were getting $13. Some blacks protested. The men of the all-black Fifty-fourth Massachusetts Regiment refused to accept discriminatory pay and would not accept any wages for a year.

Even worse, captured black soldiers were often shot or sold as slaves, instead of being treated as prisoners of war. On April 12, 1864, some 300 black troops who had been forced to surrender were massacred at Fort Pillow, Tennessee. Six days later, wounded and captured black soldiers were murdered by Confederate troops at the Battle of Poison Springs, Arkansas.

Earlier, President Lincoln had issued an order stating that for every black prisoner shot, a Confederate prisoner would be killed, and for every black prisoner sold into slavery, a Confederate prisoner would be subjected to forced labor. But black soldiers did not wait for Lincoln's retribution policy to be carried out. They fought fiercely, preferring death to surrender.

At the disastrous Battle of Olustee in Florida, an officer of the Fifty-fourth Massachusetts Regiment wrote, "We have had a fight, a licking, and a footrace. We marched 110 miles in 108 hours, and in that time had a three hour's fight. Our regiment lost one man in every five—going in five hundred strong and losing one hundred killed, wounded and missing. . . . Before going into battle [we] were double-quicked for a mile, and as [we]went in, General Seymour said, 'The day is lost; you must go in and save the corps.' We did go in and did save it, checked the enemy, held the field, and were the last to leave—and covered the retreat."

By the end of the Civil War, sixteen black soldiers had received the nation's highest award, the Congressional Medal of Honor, as did four black sailors. But black troops paid a heavy price. Dead or missing in action were 68,178, almost 20 percent of those who served. Thousands more were wounded.

The end of the Civil War, and the end of slavery marked a new beginning for American democracy. In the words of Tom Taylor, a black Civil War soldier, ". . . the old flag never did wave right. There was something wrong about it. There wasn't any star in it for the black man. . . . But since the war, it's all right. The black man has his star; it is the big one in the middle."

Reconstruction

On April 9, 1865, General Robert E. Lee surrendered to General Ulysses S. Grant at Appomattox Court House in Virginia. The Civil War was over. Although slavery had been abolished, resistance to black freedom still remained. Four million former slaves, most of them without skills, land, or money, looked to the U.S. government for help and protection. Anticipating this problem, Congress had, in March 1865, set up the Freedmen's Bureau under the administration of the U.S. Army.

In the face of tremendous opposition from defeated Confederate supporters, the Freedmen's Bureau attempted to find homes and jobs for former slaves, protect them from unfair labor contracts, and provide them with sufficient food and medicine. In addition, the bureau established forty hospitals and more than 4,000 schools in which approximately 250,000 black people eventually would enroll. In the words of Booker T. Washington, "It was a whole race trying to go to school—day schools, night schools and Sunday schools were always crowded."

Southern state legislatures tried to restrict black freedom by passing "Black Codes"—laws that denied former slaves the right to vote. They tried to keep them from testifying in court, prevent them from getting jobs, and restrict them from many public areas.

To counter this discrimination, Pennsylvania Congressman Thaddeus Stevens and Massachusetts Senator Charles Sumner urged passage of legislation to protect the rights of blacks. Under their leadership, Congress passed the Reconstruction Act of 1867. It placed ten southern states under military law and established universal male suffrage.

To reinforce the new civil rights legislation, the Fourteenth and Fifteenth Amendments to the U.S. Constitution were passed. The Fourteenth Amendment stated that anyone born in the United States was a citizen and could not be deprived of "life, liberty or property without due process of law." The Fifteenth Amendment guaranteed blacks the right to vote. The Thirteenth Amendment, which outlawed slavery, had already been passed.*

The former slaves were quick to take their new rights. Many men were elected to state government and to Congress—among them, Senators Blanche K. Bruce, Hiram R. Revels, and John R. Lynch of Mississippi and Richard Cain and Robert Smalls of South Carolina.

As a condition for readmission to the Union, all Confederate states had to adopt new state constitutions. Thanks to black legislators, these new state constitutions not only expanded voting rights of black men but also provided free public education and abolished such common criminal punishments as whipping and branding.

Again, former slaveholders fought back. The Ku Klux Klan, a white terrorist organization, sprang up in Tennessee and soon spread throughout the South. Its members beat and murdered thousands of blacks who attempted to exercise their civil rights, particularly the right to vote. As a result, U.S. soldiers were stationed at voting booths to protect blacks who wanted to vote. But in 1877, President Rutherford B. Hayes ended the Reconstruction program and withdrew federal troops from the South.

Ku Klux Klan-inspired terrorism and restriction of black voting rights eventually pushed blacks out of local and state government and resulted in the spread of "Jim Crow" laws that established segregation throughout the South. This situation continued until the civil rights movement of the 1950s and 1960s restored black voting rights and ended segregation in schools, stores, restaurants, hotels, and all public facilities.

*See pages 222-223 for the Reconstruction Amendments to the U.S. Constitution

P. B. S. Pinchback

Congressman
1837-1921

One of the most important leaders of the Reconstruction Era was Pinckney Benton Stewart Pinchback. The eighth of ten children, he was the son of a white Mississippi planter, William Pinchback, and a former slave of African, American Indian, and white ancestry. Shortly before Pinckney's birth in 1837, his mother, Eliza Stewart, and her children were sent to live in Philadelphia. When Mr. Pinchback died, Eliza Stewart and her children were denied money from his estate. To help support the family, young Pinckney went to work as a cabin boy on canal and Mississippi riverboats.

At the outbreak of Civil War, the young man offered his services to the Union army. He was assigned to recruit black soldiers but soon quit in protest over the army's discrimination against them. Taking an aggressive stand, Pinchback demanded political rights for blacks, stating that they should not be drafted if they could not vote.

At the conclusion of the war, Pinchback became active in the Republican party in Louisiana. He was a strong supporter of universal suffrage, a free public school system, and guaranteed civil rights for all people.

Elected to the Louisiana State Senate in 1868, Pinchback introduced legislation outlawing racial discrimination in public accommodations. In 1870 he established the *New Orleans Louisianian*, a newspaper that remained in operation for eleven years. In 1871 he became lieutenant governor when Oscar J. Dunn, another black legislator, died. Then, when Governor Henry Clay Warmoth was impeached, Pinchback served as acting governor until he was replaced forty-three days later.

The following year, Pinckney was elected congressman-at-large and also U. S. senator. Both elections, however, were contested. This was not uncommon. Several blacks elected to Congress were prevented from taking their seats.

In a speech that outlined many of the principles that he stood for, P. B. S. Pinchback defended his election, stating, "... several Senators ... think me a very bad man .... But of what does my badness consist? I am bad because I have dared on several important occasions to have an independent opinion. I am bad because I have dared at all times to advocate and insist on exact and equal justice to all mankind. I am bad because having colored blood in my veins, I have dared to aspire to the United States Senate .... I have been told that if I dared utter such sentiments as these in public that I certainly would be kept out of the Senate; all I have to say in answer to this is that if I cannot enter the Senate except with bated breath and on bended knees, I prefer not to enter at all."

P. B. S. Pinchback never was allowed to take his Senate seat. Instead, he was given $16,666 to cover some of the salary he would have received as an active senator. Although he was denied his seat in the House of Representatives, Congress could not deny Pinckney Pinchback's importance to the Louisiana people whose civil rights he had fought so hard to protect.

Booker T. Washington

Educator, Statesman
1856-1915

"No greater injury can be done to any youth than to let him feel that because he belongs to this or that race he will be advanced in life regardless of his own merits or efforts." — Booker T. Washington

When the Civil War ended in 1865, Booker T. Washington was nine years old. He moved to Malden, West Virginia, with his mother, a former slave, and other members of his family. There he went to work in the salt mines, where he would get up at 4:00 A.M. and work all day. At night he taught himself to read.

Wanting a better education, Washington left home in 1872 to attend Hampton Normal and Agricultural Institute in Virginia. Because he had little money, he was forced to travel most of the way on foot. Once there, he got a job as a janitor to pay for his room and board. A white benefactor paid his tuition. Four years later, he graduated with honors and was chosen to speak at the commencement.

In 1881 the Alabama legislature decided to establish a school at Tuskegee to train black teachers. Samuel C. Armstrong, the head of Hampton Institute, recommended that Washington run the new school, which was housed temporarily in an old church. Determined to make the school successful, Washington borrowed money to purchase an abandoned plantation, where students eventually built classrooms, dormitories, and a chapel and developed skills in farming, carpentry, printing, and shoemaking.

Under Washington's leadership, Tuskegee soon became a leading black institution. By 1888 it had a student body of more than 400 and owned 540 acres of land. With persistence, Washington attracted many fine black teachers to the school, including the great scientist George Washington Carver.

In his efforts to raise money for Tuskegee, Washington became friendly with many of America's leading white businessmen. In 1892 he established the National Negro Business League to encourage the development of black-owned businesses. He also wrote his autobiography, *Up From Slavery*, which became a best-seller and was translated into more than a dozen languages. Considered by many to be the most important black leader of the time, Booker T. Washington often advised presidents William Howard Taft and Theodore Roosevelt on political appointments.

Booker T. Washington believed that blacks would advance through hard work. This, he felt, would lead to respect and acceptance by the white community. He seemed to accept segregation while urging white support for black education and economic development. In a major speech in Atlanta, Georgia, he said, "The wisest among the race understand [that seeking] social equality is the extremest folly." This manner of thinking infuriated other black leaders, many of whom felt that he was ignoring the erosion of black political and civil rights in order to promote black economic development.

Privately, Washington was more concerned with the increasing threats to black rights than his white supporters or black critics realized. He paid the legal fees of several lawyers working to overturn segregation and voting discrimination laws. And he used his position to maintain black influence in the Republican party in the South.

In spite of the criticism he received from some black leaders, Booker T. Washington was admired by black people throughout the country. He spent his life preaching hard work and perseverance. By practicing what he preached, he turned Tuskegee into a model for other black schools and had a major impact on future black education.

Nat Love

Cowboy, Range Rider
1854-1921

His real name was Nat Love, a former slave from Tennessee. But as a result of a book based on his life, he became known as Deadwood Dick. He was a gunfighter, scout, range boss, rodeo rider, and, to hear him tell it, the best all-around cowboy in the West. He survived outlaw attacks, capture by Indians, and fourteen gunshot wounds. Although he often went drinking with his friend Bat Masterson, legend has it he also rode his horse into a saloon one day and ordered two whiskeys—one for himself and one for his horse.

Nat Love's adventures began in 1869 when he got lucky and won a horse in a raffle. As a teenager, he spent most of his time sharecropping to support his sisters and widowed mother. But after he won the raffle, a new life opened up for him. He sold his horse, split the money with his mother, paid a few bills, and took off for Dodge City, Kansas, to become a cowboy.

Already an experienced horse trainer, Love quickly learned to herd and brand cattle and to use a gun. He got his first job at the Duval ranch. Later, he hired on with the Peter Gallinger outfit.

In 1876 a big Fourth of July celebration was held in Deadwood, South Dakota. The town was crowded with cowboys from all over the territory. It was during this celebration that Love competed in several contests and made his claim to fame. He won the rifle and handgun matches and set a record in the rope throw and bronco-riding contest.

As the West became settled, Love left range life and took a job on the railroad. He was like thousands of other black men and women who had left behind memories of slavery and traveled west seeking a fresh start.

It is estimated that 20 percent of America's cowboys were black men seeking to make a new life for themselves. As pioneers, they played a major part in settling the West and making life easier for thousands of people who came later.

The Shores family homesteading in Custer County, Nebraska, 1887

Jan Ernst Matzeliger

Inventor
1852-1889

"If the shoe fits," it's partly because a man named Jan Matzeliger invented a wonderful machine that knocked shoe manufacturers right off their feet.

Jan Matzeliger was born in Paramaribo, Suriname (then called Dutch Guiana), in South America. His mother was a native black from Suriname and his father was a wealthy Dutch engineer from Holland. At age ten, Jan went to work in a machine shop. When he was nineteen, he got a job on an East Indian merchant ship and spent the next two years at sea. When the ship docked in Philadelphia, he decided to give life in the United States a try.

After working at various jobs in Philadelphia, Matzeliger moved to Boston in 1876 and, a year later, settled in Lynn, Massachusetts, where he got a job with a shoe manufacturing company. Meanwhile, he started night school to study physics and improve his English. In his spare time, he painted and gave art lessons.

As Matzeliger worked in the shoe manufacturing company, he noticed that production was slow because workers had to attach the bottom of the shoe to the top by hand. So he decided to invent a machine that could perform this task. Within six months, he had built his first model from wood, wire, and cigar boxes. Although it was far from perfect, it was impressive enough to attract a $50 offer, which he rejected.

In 1880 Matzeliger completed a more advanced model. This one got him a $1,500 offer. Although he needed the money, he turned down the offer again and began work on a third model. He soon realized, however, that he would need financial help. He got it from Melville S. Nichols and Charles H. Delnow, in exchange for a two-thirds interest in his machines.

On March 20, 1883, Matzeliger received patent no. 274,207 for a "Lasting Machine" that would rapidly stitch the leather of a shoe to the sole. The drawings of it were so complicated that a scientist from the patent office in Washington, D.C., had to travel to Lynn to observe the machine in action before he could understand it. But it was worth the trip. Jan Matzeliger's lasting machine made it possible to turn out 150 to 700 pairs of shoes a day, instead of only fifty pairs a day previously. It also cut the manufacturing costs in half.

Anticipating success, Matzeliger, Nichols, and Delnow established the Union Lasting Machine Company and went into business. Soon, they sold out to a larger company. Matzeliger sold all his patents (five by this time) in return for stock in the company.

In 1886 Matzeliger became ill with tuberculosis and died three years later at the age of thirty-seven. He left his stock in the Union Lasting Machine Company to the North Congregational Church, the one church in Lynn that had not rejected him because of race. As for the company that owned his patents, it became the United Shoe Machinery Corporation. Sixty-five years later, it was worth over a billion dollars.

So, the next time you go for a walk, you might remember that it was the skill and inventiveness of Jan Ernst Matzeliger that enabled the entire U.S. shoe manufacturing industry to step out in front and put its best foot forward.

George Jordan

Soldier
1847-1904

On the night of May 13, 1880, George Jordan, a black soldier in charge of twenty-five black troopers, received word that a small white settlement located near the Mescalero Indian Reservation in New Mexico was in serious danger of attack. Ordering his men to mount up, Jordan and his group rode through the night to reach the settlement.

Once there, the troopers erected a stockade for the protection of the settlers, positioned themselves for combat, and waited. At sunset, 100 Apache Indians attacked. Although they were outnumbered four to one, Jordan and his men drove off the Indians. Regrouping, the Apaches charged again. Forced back a second time, the Indians finally rode off and never returned.

Born in Williamson County, Kentucky, George Jordan lived there until 1866 when he enlisted in the newly established Ninth Cavalry. The Ninth Cavalry was one of four all-black military units operating in the West. Two of them, the famous Twenty-fourth and Twenty-fifth regiments, were infantry. The other two, the Ninth and Tenth, were cavalry. Made up mainly of experienced Civil War veterans, Indians nicknamed them Buffalo Soldiers. Famous for their courage and fighting ability, these black soldiers made up 20 percent—one out of every five—of the cavalrymen in the Old West.

In addition to serving in the West, these regiments also saw action during the Spanish-American War. Soldiers from the Ninth and Tenth

Cavalry are often credited with saving the day for Theodore Roosevelt's Rough Riders at the Battles of San Juan Hill and Las Guasimas. Said a white southern officer, "If it had not been for the Negro cavalry, the Rough Riders would have been exterminated . . . the Negroes saved that fight." And Teddy Roosevelt said, "I don't think that any Rough Rider will ever forget the tie that binds us to the Ninth and Tenth Cavalry."

George Jordan served faithfully with the army for thirty years and participated in numerous campaigns against American Indians, Mexican bandits, and American outlaws. He received the Congressional Medal of Honor for the leadership and courage he demonstrated in 1880 when he fought the Apache in New Mexico.

During his last years on active duty, Jordan was stationed at Fort Robinson, Nebraska. Following his retirement, he moved to Crawford, Nebraska, where he became a leader in the black community.

When he became sick in 1904, he returned to Fort Robinson for medical help. But the army doctor refused to treat him, saying there was no room in the hospital. George Jordan died a few days later.

Although the army treated George Jordan badly, history does not. Today, George Jordan, along with other Buffalo Soldiers, takes his place among America's most courageous fighting men.

Lewis Howard Latimer

Inventor
1848-1928

When Alexander Graham Bell applied for a patent on his telephone in 1876, the blueprints he submitted to illustrate his invention were drawn by Lewis Howard Latimer, a young black draftsman.

Born in Chelsea, Massachusetts, in 1848, Lewis Howard Latimer was raised in Boston. When he was only ten his father deserted the family, and Lewis was forced to quit school and go to work.

After the Civil War, he got a job as an office boy for Crosby and Gould, a legal firm specializing in patent law. Investors, hoping to acquire patents protecting the rights to their inventions, paid Crosby and Gould to provide drawings of the inventions. As a result, Crosby and Gould employed a number of draftsmen—artists who specialize in drawing inventions.

Drafting fascinated Latimer. He bought a set of secondhand drafting tools and, with the help of library books and advice from other draftsmen, learned the trade. Feeling confident in his ability, he submitted some of his drawings to Crosby and Gould. They were impressed, and in a short time, Lewis had progressed from junior draftsman to chief draftsman.

One day Lewis met Alexander Graham Bell. A friendship developed, and Bell asked Latimer to make the drawings for his telephone. Then in 1880 Latimer became a draftsman for the United States Electric Lighting Company in Bridgeport, Connecticut. In addition to illustrating the work of others, he began working on inventions of his own.

Lewis Latimer became fascinated with the new electric light process, and, in 1881, along with Joseph V. Nichols, he received a patent for the Latimer Lamp. It utilized a greatly improved method of manufacturing the carbon filaments that give off the light in a light bulb. As a result of Latimer's invention, he was called upon to supervise the installation of electric light plants in New York City and the creation of an incandescent light division for the Maxim-Weston Electric Company in London, England.

In 1884 Latimer became a member of the Edison Pioneers—a small, select group of scientists who worked closely with Thomas Edison. When Lewis Latimer died in 1928, they said of him, "We hardly mourn his inevitable going so much as we rejoice in pleasant memory at having been associated with him in a great work for all people."

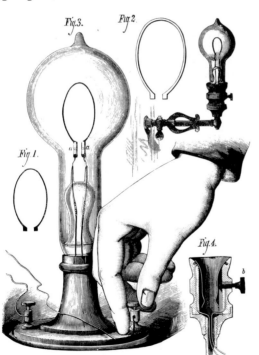

Latimer's electric lamp, patented September 13, 1881, improved the method of manufacturing electricity.

Scott Joplin

Pianist, Composer
1868-1917

In the years following the Civil War, scores of black musicians traveled throughout the country, playing in churches and saloons, trying to earn enough money to eat. Building on old African rhythms, they developed new musicial forms that were uniquely American. One of these musicians, Scott Joplin, became the leading composer of ragtime music.

Born in Texarkana, Texas, in 1868, Scott Joplin grew up playing piano in houses where his mother, Florence Joplin, worked as a maid. Word of his exceptional talent soon spread throughout the community, and a German music teacher offered to give young Scott formal training.

Within a short time, Joplin was playing in churches as well as for social events. Shortly after his mother died, he left home to become a professional musician. As he traveled across the country, he was attracted to ragtime—a rapidly growing form of black music that had evolved from the old slave songs. Drawing on African traditions, ragtime combined a syncopated or varied rhythm pattern with the melody. This was known as "ragging" the melody and was popular especially in dance music. In fact, dances were often called rags.

In 1895 Scott moved to St. Louis and got a job playing piano at "Honest" John Turpin's Silver Dollar Saloon. Several years later he settled in Sedalia, Missouri, where he began to study and write music. During the day, Scott took courses in music theory at George R. Smith

College. At night, he played piano in the Maple Leaf Club.

In 1899 Scott published "Original Rags," a beautifully crafted work. Later, he took another piece, "Maple Leaf Rag" (named for the club where he worked), to two publishers. Both rejected it. Both made a big mistake. Fortunately, a music dealer named John Stark heard the piece and printed it.

Within a few months, "Maple Leaf Rag" had sold more than 600,000 copies. Considered by many to be the best rag ever written, it became the first piece of sheet music to sell more than a million copies. Its publication brought worldwide demand for ragtime music, which lasted until the end of World War I.

The publication of "Maple Leaf Rag" brought Joplin financial security. It allowed him to quit playing in saloons and concentrate on teaching and writing music. Although none of his later work had the financial success of "Maple Leaf Rag," it was of excellent quality.

But Scott Joplin wasn't satisfied. He wanted to write opera. His first attempt, *The Guest of Honor*, closed after only a few performances. But it was a work called *Treemonisha* that was closer to his heart. Written partly in tribute to his mother, Joplin was determined to see *Treemonisha* performed on stage. Because he couldn't find backers, he decided to produce it himself. All of his efforts, however, were in vain. The audience didn't understand or appreciate the opera, and it closed. Joplin was devastated.

In 1916 he was committed to Manhattan State Hospital, where he died the following April. At the time of his death, ragtime was fading in popularity. Young people, thinking it was old-fashioned, were now more interested in jazz. But Scott Joplin's music was too good to be forgotten. In the 1970s, "The Entertainer" was chosen as the theme song for the Academy Award-winning movie *The Sting*, and his opera *Treemonisha* was dusted off and finally produced on Broadway, where it became a hit. It was fitting tribute to the man music experts call the "King of Ragtime."

George Washington Williams

Soldier, Lawyer, Historian
1849-1891

At age fourteen, George Washington Williams joined the Union army to fight slavery in America. When he died, at age forty-two, he was trying to end slavery in Africa. In between, he served in the Mexican army, and was a minister, a lawyer, a politician, a newspaperman, and one of the best Afro-American historians this country has ever produced.

George Williams's career started during the Civil War when he lied about his age and joined the Sixth Massachusetts Regiment under his uncle's name. The army soon discovered the truth and put him out. Not long afterward, Williams reenlisted and became a sergeant major on the staff of General N. P. Jackson. Fighting in several battles, he was wounded in a skirmish near Fort Harrison, Virginia, in 1864 and was discharged a year later.

Williams then joined the Mexican army. He resigned after about a year and enlisted in the U.S. Tenth Cavalry. This time, he took part in the campaign against the Comanche Indians, was wounded, and received a medical discharge.

Having had enough of military life, Williams decided to become a minister. He enrolled at the Newton Theological Institution in Massachusetts and graduated in 1874. The following year, he became an ordained minister and served as pastor of the Twelfth Street Church in Boston. But after a year, he moved to Washington, D.C., where he started a newspaper called *The Commoner.* Even though the paper had the support of such people as Frederick Douglass, it eventually failed. In 1876 Williams settled in Cincinnati, where he resumed his ministry at the Union Baptist Church.

Once again, one career was not enough for him. Besides becoming a journalist and writing for several newspapers, he began to study law. In 1879 he was admitted to the bar and was elected to the Ohio legislature.

Politics, however, did not hold Williams for long, either. While continuing to serve as a legislator, he began collecting information on the history of black people in the United States. After extensive research, he wrote an impressive two-volume book called *History of the Negro Race in America from 1619 to 1880*. Published in 1883, it became the first extensive work of its kind by a black American and was an immediate success. Five years later, his second book, *History of the Negro Troops in the War of Rebellion*, was published. This, too, was widely praised.

As a result of his successful books, Williams became a popular lecturer and made several trips to Europe. On one of these trips, he met King Leopold II of Belgium who convinced him to help develop the Congo Free State in Africa. Soon, Williams discovered that the Congo was not a free state but a colony owned by the king.

Unfortunately for Leopold, Williams became so interested in the Congo that he decided to visit it. The trip proved to be a tremendous shock for him. Although Leopold said he was opposed to slavery, Williams found that the Congolese were treated like slaves. Forced to work long hours on the rubber plantations, they were subjected to terrible punishments when they failed to produce enough.

Outraged by what he saw, Williams wrote *An Open Letter to His Serene Majesty, Leopold II, King of the Belgians*. In it, he denounced the king and his rule in Africa. The report made a strong impact not only in Belgium but also in the United States, France, and England. An international campaign to end the cruel conditions in the Congo resulted. Williams then followed up with two more reports and an investigation of the Portuguese and British colonies in Africa. He was working on another report on the Congo Free State when he became ill and died in 1891.

George Washington Williams, who at age fourteen had joined the army to fight for black freedom in the United States, died fighting for black freedom in Africa.

Cartoon published in 1906 depicts Leopold and the Congo "Free" State.

George Washington Carver

Agricultural Scientist
1861-1943

"Education is the key to unlock the golden door of freedom . . ." — George W. Carver

Most people just eat peanuts; George Washington Carver developed 325 different products from them, including coffee, face powder, ink, butter, shampoo, vinegar, soap, and wood stains.

George Carver was born of slave parents in 1861 on a plantation belonging to Moses and Susan Carver near Diamond, Missouri. When he was just a baby, he and his mother were kidnapped by night riders and taken to Arkansas. Within a short time, George was returned to the Carver plantation, but his mother was never found. A sickly child, he was unable to do heavy work and, instead, spent much of his time wandering in the nearby woods collecting flowers and plants.

After the Civil War, he and his brother James continued to live on the Carver plantation, where he taught himself to read. At age ten, he left the plantation. For the next few years, he worked at odd jobs and attended school wherever he could. Finally, he enrolled at Minneapolis High School in Kansas and won a scholarship to attend Highland University. When he showed up at Highland, however, the school refused to admit him because he was black.

But Carver was not discouraged. He continued to work and save money. Years later, he was accepted at Simpson College in Iowa and supported himself by ironing clothes for fellow students.

Although Carver was artistically inclined, he was more interested in science. With the help of his art teacher, he was accepted at Iowa Agricultural College in 1891. His work in botany and chemistry was so outstanding that, upon graduation, he was asked to stay on as an assistant instructor and director of the greenhouse. While teaching, Carver continued his own research. He conducted important investigations into several varieties of fungus that were attacking wheat, soybeans, oats, blackberries, and maple trees.

In 1896 he received a letter from Booker T. Washington, founder of Tuskegee Institute in Alabama, asking him to work there. Tuskegee was a poor school and could not offer him much in the way of salary or laboratory equipment. Nevertheless, Carver agreed to go.

At Tuskegee, Carver developed a system of crop rotation. He planted a legume crop (such as peanuts, which replenish minerals in the soil) one year, followed by a crop of cotton the next year. Its purpose was to keep the soil rich and improve the harvest. This system became so successful that an oversupply of peanuts resulted. Carver responded by coming up with more than two dozen uses for them. Soon, farmers were making more money raising peanuts than harvesting cotton.

While continuing to develop uses for the peanut, Carver began to experiment with the sweet potato. Before long, he had discovered 118 products that could be made from it, including dyes, ink, and synthetic rubber. As his work progressed, he was visited by the crown prince of Sweden and the British Prince of Wales. Thomas Edison asked him to join his staff at a yearly salary of more than $100,000. And autombile manufacturer Henry Ford also made him a generous offer. But Carver preferred to remain at Tuskegee.

Unconcerned about money or material possessions, Carver concentrated on his research, hoping to improve the lives of black farmers. ". . . It has always been the one great ideal of my life," he said, "to be of the greatest good to the greatest number of my people."

Granville T. Woods

Inventor
1856-1910

Known as "The Black Edison," Granville T. Woods was a brilliant inventor of electromechanical devices. He received more than sixty patents during his lifetime for inventions ranging from a telephone transmitter to an electrically heated egg incubator.

Woods was born in Columbus, Ohio, in 1856. At age ten, he was forced to quit school and go to work. By sixteen, he had moved to Missouri, where he worked as a fireman and an engineer on the railroads. Then he moved to New York City, where he studied electrical engineering while working as an engineer on the British steamship *Ironsides.*

Returning to Ohio in 1884, Granville and his brother Lyates opened a machine shop in Cincinnati and began manufacturing telephone, telegraph, and electrical equipment. The same year, he received his first patent for an improved telephone transmitter. The American Bell Telephone Company of Boston quickly bought the rights to it.

In 1885 Woods invented a device that combined features of the telephone and the telegraph. By 1887 he had patented seven more machines, one of which could telegraph messages to moving trains, warning railroad personnel of dangers on the tracks.

Over the next fifteen years, he patented an amazing array of inventions: electromagnetic brakes, an automatic safety cutoff for electrical circuits, a light dimmer, an overhead conducting system for trolley cars, and an electrified "third rail" that became an important element of subway systems.

Of the more than sixty patents credited to Granville Woods, many were sold to such companies as General Electric, Westinghouse, and American Bell Telephone. Unfortunately, he died in poverty, much of his money having been lost to legal fees resulting from a libel suit brought against him when he charged an American Engineering Company manager with stealing patents.

Few scientists can match the genius of Granville T. Woods. His inventions modernized the transportation system in the United States and improved the uses of electricity. Called "The Black Edison," his work provided a spark that moved the electronics and transportation industries forward.

New York City in the 1890s

Daniel Hale Williams

Physician, Educator

1856-1931

Today we speak of heart transplants and artificial hearts. In 1893 people were talking about the world's first successful heart operation and the surgeon who did it—Daniel Hale Williams.

The patient was a man named James Cornish who had been stabbed in the heart and left for dead. He was brought to Chicago's Provident Hospital where, without the aid of penicillin, antibiotics, or X rays, Dr. Williams performed what many believed was a medical miracle. He actually sewed up a torn heart.

Born in Hollidaysburg, Pennsylvania, on January 18, 1856, Williams went to work at age twelve as an apprentice to a shoemaker. During the next few years, he worked at various jobs, always hoping that he could return to school someday.

At sixteen, he graduated from Haire's Classical Academy in Wisconsin and became an apprentice to Dr. Henry Palmer. Then he entered Chicago Medical College. Graduating in only three years, he set up practice in Chicago and joined the surgical staff at the South Side Dispensary. He also became an instructor at Chicago Medical College and, in 1889, was appointed to the Illinois State Board of Health.

Concerned that there was no hospital for blacks in Chicago, Dr. Williams established the Provident Hospital and Training Association in 1891. It provided hospital care for everyone and training for black physicians and nurses. It was here, in Provident Hospital, that Dr. Williams sewed up James Cornish's heart.

The operation made news all over the world. When President Grover Cleveland heard about it, he asked Dr. Willliams to become chief surgeon at Freedman's Hospital in Washington, D.C. Dr. Williams accepted and immediately began reorganizing it. He also created a training program for black nurses and doctors.

During the Spanish American War, Dr. Williams evaluated and selected surgeons for military service. After the war, he resumed his research and lectured on the need for expanded medical facilities for blacks. When he finally retired in 1926, he had helped to establish at least forty hospitals primarily serving black patients.

Physician, scientist, and educator, Dr. Daniel Hale Williams contributed enormously to the development of surgical theory and practice and greatly expanded medical care and career opportunities for black people.

Chicago Provident Hospital at Thirty-sixth and Dearborn Streets

Madame C. J. Walker

Cosmetics Manufacturer, Humanitarian
1867-1919

"I am a woman who came from the cotton fields of the South.... I promoted myself into the business of manufacturing hair goods and preparations.... I have built my own factory on my own ground."
—Madame C. J. Walker

Most people's dreams are forgotten quickly; Madame C. J. Walker turned hers into a million dollars.

Born Sarah Breedlove to former slaves in Louisiana in 1867, she was orphaned at age five. At fourteen, she married a man named McWilliams. But six years later, he died, leaving her alone to raise their daughter A'Lelia.

After moving to St. Louis, Missouri, Sarah McWilliams, as she was known then, found work as a washerwoman. While working hard to educate her daughter, Ms. McWilliams's hair began falling out. Although she tried various remedies, nothing seemed to help. Then one night, she dreamed about an old man who showed her things to mix up for her hair. When she awoke, she gave the formula a try. After combining the various ingredients, she tested the mixture on herself. The result: "My hair was coming in faster than it had ever fallen out," she said. "I tried it on my friends; it helped them. I made up my mind that I would sell it."

In July 1905, Sarah McWilliams moved to Denver, Colorado. Six months later, she married a newspaperman named Charles Walker and began calling herself Madame C. J. Walker, the name by which she is known today. She began to travel widely, demonstrating her beauty preparations, and in 1908 opened a second office in Pittsburgh. Walker advertised extensively in black newspapers and, in 1910, was able to establish her own factory in Indianapolis. By then her company was earning $7,000 a week.

During this time, black women were among the lowest paid workers in America. Victimized by both race and sex discrimination, those not working as sharecroppers or on farms were employed mainly as domestic workers and washerwomen. For the approximately 5,000 black women working for Madame Walker, there was better pay, greater opportunity, and more dignity. She insisted that "loveliness" was linked to "cleanliness" rather than race. In a society where white skin and Caucasian features were the standard for beauty, Walker's assertion, that black women were beautiful, helped many change their self-image.

Always concerned about the black community, Madame Walker organized her women agents into "Walker Clubs" and provided cash prizes for outstanding community service. She contributed generously for scholarships to Tuskegee, to the National Association for the Advancement of Colored People, and to other black charities both in the United States and abroad. She helped direct a fund-raising drive to establish Mary McLeod Bethune's school in Daytona and donated the money needed to pay off the mortgage on Frederick Douglass's home.

A woman of determination, energy, and vision, Madame C. J. Walker became America's first black woman millionaire when she followed her dream to become a hair restorer and came out ahead.

Charles Young

Soldier
1864-1922

"I am always willing to aid in any work for the good of the country in general and our race in particular." — Charles Young

He was the third black man to graduate from West Point and the first to serve as a U.S. military attaché. Charles Young was born in a log cabin in Mayslick, Kentucky. He graduated from West Point in 1889 and was assigned to Fort Robinson, Nebraska, where he joined the famous Ninth Cavalry. After serving there for four years, he was transferred to Fort Du Chesne, Utah, and was later selected to teach French, mathematics, tactics, and military science at Wilberforce University in Ohio.

When the Spanish-American War began, Young was placed in command of the Ninth Ohio Volunteer Infantry and sent to Cuba. In 1901 he was transferred to the Philippines, where his men nicknamed him "Follow Me" because of his courage and leadership.

Because of his distinguished military record, Young was made military attaché to Haiti and the Dominican Republic in 1904. While serving as attaché, he explored Haiti and sent back lengthy reports on the country and its people. He also made detailed maps of previously uncharted areas. Young's diplomatic accomplishments were due in part to his interest in different people and cultures and to his readiness to learn. He spoke Latin, Greek, German, French, Spanish, and Italian; played the piano and the violin; and composed poetry. While in Haiti, he wrote a book called *Military Morale of Nations and Races*, an English-French-Creole dictionary, and a play.

As a result of his diplomatic success in Haiti, Young was assigned as military attaché to Liberia. As he had done previously in Haiti, he charted maps of the country and studied the native culture. Often, it was dangerous work. One time, while on a mission to rescue an American officer who had been ambushed by Gola tribesmen, he was shot and wounded in the right arm.

After returning from Liberia, Young served with General John J. Pershing in Mexico. He established a school for black enlisted men at Fort Hauchucha, hoping that many of them would later be able to qualify for officer's training.

At the outbreak of World War I, Colonel Young looked forward to commanding black troops in Europe. He was denied a command, however, when army doctors diagnosed him as suffering from high blood pressure and an advanced case of nephritis (Bright's disease). Believing that his denial of command was racially motivated, Young rode his horse all the way from Ohio to Washington, D.C., to prove that he was fit for combat. It didn't help. Though he protested bitterly, he was forced to retire from active duty on June 22, 1917. But in 1919 the State Department asked him to return to Africa as a special adviser to the Liberian government. Three years later, he died of nephritis while on a visit to Lagos, Nigeria.

Colonel Charles Young served in the army at a time when black men were generally regarded as unfit to be high-ranking officers. The nine black men appointed to West Point before him had faced tremendous hostility and prejudice. Only two had graduated. In the U.S. Armed Forces black troops were routinely placed under the command of white officers. In the face of such opposition, the fact that Colonel Young graduated from West Point and achieved high military rank was an amazing accomplishment.

Elijah McCoy

Inventor
1843-1929

When Elijah McCoy's parents escaped from slavery in Kentucky via the Underground Railroad, they didn't know that one day they would have a son whose inventions would affect railroad transportation all over the world.

Born in Canada in 1843, Elijah McCoy was the third of twelve children. After attending school near his home, his parents sent him to Edinburgh, Scotland, where he studied mechanical engineering. Moving to Detroit to find work, he was forced to take a job as a fireman on the Michigan Central Railroad, when prejudice kept him from being hired as an engineer.

In those days, trains and other machinery were stopped every day to be oiled. Recognizing that this was a great waste of time and money, McCoy started the Elijah McCoy Manufacturing Company in Detroit, Michigan, and developed a device that would lubricate machinery automatically while it was still in operation. In 1872 he received a U.S. government patent for his steam engine lubricator, the "lubricator cup."

But McCoy didn't stop there. He kept improving his device and developing variations of it. In time, he received forty-two patents for inventions and saved millions of dollars. Soon his systems were in use all over the world.

Although others tried to copy his work, people continued to demand the original. Using a phrase that has now become part of the American language, people said they wanted the "Real McCoy."

Ida B. Wells-Barnett

Journalist,
Civil Rights Leader
1862-1931

"Christian and moral forces . . . should insist that . . . this nation do its duty to exalt justice and preserve inviolate the sacredness of human life." — Ida B. Wells

I t was called "A Red Record"—the first complete list of lynchings in the United States during a three-year period—and the bloody title fit. In the ten years from 1890 to 1900 1,217 blacks were murdered by lynch mobs. Compiled by Ida Wells-Barnett in 1895, this report set the tone for her life-long crusade against lynching.

Born a slave in Holly Springs, Mississippi, Ida Wells struggled to gain an education. When she was sixteen, both of her parents died within twenty-four hours of each other. Lying about her age, Wells became a teacher and the sole support of five brothers and sisters. Her pay was $25 a month.

In 1884 she moved to Memphis, where she continued to teach. When she complained of poor conditions in the school, however, she was fired.

In the meantime, she had begun writing for the *Living Way* newspaper. Then, with a little money she had managed to save, she bought an interest in the Memphis *Free Speech* newspaper, which also carried her work. Within nine months, subscriptions to the *Free Speech* increased by 2,000. Threats against her life also increased.

Nonetheless, when three black men were dragged from jail in 1892 and lynched, Ida Wells did more than complain. She named names—

men who were directly involved and city officials who refused to take action. She also wrote articles urging blacks to boycott the new street-car line and, if possible, to leave the city entirely. Within two months, approximately 2,000 blacks had moved away and the streetcar company was almost bankrupt.

At the time, many people accepted lynching as a satisfactory way of punishing black criminals. But Wells knew that the men who were lynched in Memphis were not criminals. They had been killed because they had set up a successful grocery store that was taking business away from a competing white-owned store. If the men hanged in Memphis had been innocent, thought Wells, then many other lynch victims might have been innocent as well.

Determined to uncover the truth, she began traveling across the country, interviewing eyewitnesses and visiting the scene of various lynchings. Of the 728 murders she investigated, she found that only one-third involved blacks actually accused of crimes, let alone convicted of them. Most lynch victims were murdered for "quarreling with whites," for "making threats," or because of "race prejudice." Not only men but even women and children had been murdered by mobs.

Ida Wells continued to write editorials attacking those who offered excuses for lynch mobs. One day, she went a little too far, and an angry mob retaliated by burning her newspaper office. Luckily, she was out of town when it happened, but, thereafter, she was no longer safe in Memphis. She moved to New York, where she continued to make herself heard.

On June 5, 1892 the *New York Age* carried a long article written by Wells. In it, she gave names, dates, places, and brutal details of hundreds of lynchings. Ten thousand copies of the paper were sold, including 1,000 in Memphis alone. In addition to writing, she traveled to England to gain support for her antilynching campaign.

In 1895 Wells married lawyer and editor Ferdinand Lee Barnett.

With his support, she organized women's clubs and political groups committed to helping blacks. Her work in stressing the need for a national black organization was instrumental in the founding of the National Association for the Advancement of Colored People (NAACP) in 1909.

In her unceasing struggle to outlaw lynching, Ida Wells-Barnett faced the difficult and often dangerous task of trying to change people's thinking as well as their behavior. Because of her efforts, lynching is regarded now as a vicious crime that no decent person can ignore, justify, or excuse.

Mary Church Terrell

Women's Rights Advocate, Educator
1863-1954

The same murder that started Ida Wells-Barnett on her anti-lynching crusade also triggered a change in the life of Mary Church Terrell. One of the murder victims had been her close friend. When Mary Terrell heard the news, she called on Frederick Douglass to help arrange a meeting with President Benjamin Harrison. Together, Terrell and Douglass pleaded with Harrison to condemn lynching in his annual message to Congress. When he refused, Terrell took it upon herself to begin a lifelong struggle to wipe out lynching, racism, and sexism.

Mary Terrell was the daughter of Robert Church, a former slave who had become wealthy in real estate. In 1884 she graduated from Oberlin College in Ohio and then went on to get her masters degree in 1888. Much to the displeasure of her father, who thought women should not work, she became an instructor at Wilberforce University. "He disinherited me," she said, "[and] refused to write to me for a year because I went to Wilberforce to teach. Further, I was ridiculed and told that no man would want to marry a woman who studied higher mathematics. I said I'd take a chance and run the risk." As it turned out, Mary Church eventually married Robert Terrell, who later became a judge in the municipal court of the District of Columbia.

Her marriage forced her to turn down an opportunity to become registrar at Oberlin College in 1891, but in 1895 she was appointed to the Board of Education in Washington, D.C., becoming the first black woman in the country to hold such a position. In spite of her personal success, Mrs. Terrell faced an uphill battle because many people felt women were intellectually and emotionally inferior to men.

She worked closely with white suffragette leaders Susan B. Anthony and Jane Addams. They were campaigning to win passage of the Nineteenth Amendment to the Constitution, which would give women the right to vote. It was a rocky alliance. The white women's groups were often quick to ignore or deny black rights if they felt that to do otherwise would cost them support, especially in the South.

Entry of the United States into World War I had a major impact on black women. As many whites entered the army or found better paying jobs in defense industries, thousands of blacks moved north to take their place. Although the pay was better in the North, blacks generally did not have the protection of the largely white organized labor movement. To improve working conditions and to obtain equal treatment for black women, Terrell helped form the Women Wage-Earners Association. It organized black domestic workers, waitresses, nurses, and tobacco stemmers. She also helped establish the National Association of Colored Women (NACW) and was a founder of the NAACP.

Mary Church Terrell remained active all of her life. At age eighty-six, she began a three-year battle against the American Association of University Women because they refused to admit black women. She also led an economic boycott of Washington, D.C., department stores that refused to serve blacks. Even at age ninety, she was marching at the head of a picket line to end segregation in restaurants.

Like other black women leaders, Mary Church Terrell demanded respect not only for herself but also for black women everywhere. At a time when women as a group were treated with condescension, and black women often were treated with contempt, Mary Church Terrell's was one of the few voices raised on their behalf.

Matthew Henson

Explorer
1866-1955

"Great ideals are the glory of man alone. . . . Only man can get a vision and an inspiration that will lift him above the level of himself and send him forth against all opposition. . . to do and to dare and to accomplish wonderful and great things for the world and for humanity." Those words are from the lecture notes of Matthew Henson, a man who started life near the bottom of society and ended up at the very top of the world as the first person ever to reach the North Pole.

Born in Charles County, Maryland, Matthew Alexander Henson lost his mother when he was only two years old. Six years later, his father died. For a while, Matthew attended school in Washington, D.C., where he lived with an uncle. But around the age of twelve, he ran away to Baltimore and signed on as a cabin boy on the merchant ship *Katie Hinds.* The ship's commander, Captain Childs, took a liking to the boy, and he spent the next six years sailing around the world with him. By the time Henson was eighteen, he had traveled across the Atlantic and Pacific oceans, the China and Baltic seas, and through the Straits of Magellan at the tip of South America.

Returning to Washington, D.C., Matthew Henson got a job in a clothing store as a clerk. One day in 1887, a naval officer, Robert E. Peary, entered the store. He said he was planning an expedition to explore building a canal through Nicaragua that would link the Atlantic and Pacific oceans.

Impressed with Matthew Henson, Peary hired him. His seagoing experience and his ability to chart a path through jungle terrain made him a valuable associate. The Nicaragua expedition marked the beginning of an association between the two men that would last for more than twenty years.

Robert Peary wanted to be the first man to reach the North Pole. It was a dream Matthew Henson soon came to share. He learned to speak the Eskimo language and became skilled in making sledges and other equipment needed in the regions of the far north. Together, he and Peary made seven trips to the Arctic. Six times, ice, storms, and sub-zero temperatures forced them to turn back.

In 1908 they set out on their final expedition. Peary was accompanied by several other white assistants and Eskimo guides. But it was Matthew Henson who was assigned to lead the first dog sled. "He is a better dog driver," said Peary, "and can handle a sledge better than any man living except some of the best Eskimo hunters. I couldn't get along without him."

Six dog teams left Crane City, Greenland, at the edge of the Arctic Circle, established camps, and left supplies. One by one, they returned to Cape Columbia on Canada's Ellesmere Island, where they reunited for the final trek of their 478-mile journey to the North Pole.

Often, travel was unbearable. Temperatures dropped as low as 60 degrees below zero. According to Henson, "We [traveled] eighteen to twenty hours out of every twenty-four . . . . Forced marches all the time [because] we couldn't carry food for more than fifty days, fifty-five at a pinch."

Henson moved out in front, his dog team covering thirty-five miles on the first day. Peary followed, not moving as quickly because he had had several toes amputated nine years earlier because of frostbite.

On the morning of April 6, 1909, Matthew Henson reached 90 degrees north latitude. With the help of two Eskimo assistants, he built an igloo and waited for Commander Peary to arrive and confirm his calculations. After Peary arrived, the crew spent about thirty hours making observations and taking soundings before planting an American flag and packing up their gear for the long, freezing trip home.

When Henson returned from the expedition, he was so thin his wife didn't even recognize him. Few people were willing to recognize his achievements, either. Not until thirty-six years later was he awarded the Congressional Medal of Honor. Six years after Matthew Henson's death in 1955, the State House of Annapolis, Maryland, finally had a commemorative plaque designed, honoring him as co-discoverer of the North Pole.

Matthew Henson (center) holding the polar flag at the North Pole, 1909

Mary McLeod Bethune

Educator,
Civil Rights Activist
1875-1955

In 1904 Mary McLeod Bethune left home with $1.50 in her pocket and a dream of establishing a school for black children. A few months later, she made a down payment on a former garbage dump, in Daytona, Florida, where she set up the Daytona Normal and Industrial School. Tuition was fifty cents a week, and the student body consisted of five girls and Mary Bethune's son Albert. But within two years, there were 250 students. The school, which later would become the Bethune-Cookman College, was firmly established.

Born in a small cabin near Mayesville, South Carolina, Mary McLeod was the fifteenth of seventeen children. She spent her childhood working: picking cotton and washing and ironing clothes. For six years she walked five miles to and from school each day. At night, she would teach her brothers and sisters what she had learned.

Mary studied hard. She won a scholarship to Scotia Seminary in Concord, North Carolina, and later went to the Moody Bible Institute in Chicago, Illinois. Graduating in 1895, she became a teacher. Two years later, she married a fellow teacher, Albertus Bethune, and they moved to Florida, where she hoped to set up her own school.

Mary Bethune organized concerts and wrote articles in order to raise money for her school. She rode her bicycle to churches, clubs, and organizations, asking for contributions. One day, she asked a wealthy businessman, James M. Gamble of Proctor and Gamble, for support. When he visited the small shack that was her classroom, he was shocked. "Where is the school?" he asked. "It is in my mind and in my soul," Mrs. Bethune replied. Gamble was so impressed by her reply that he donated $150.

In 1935 Mrs. Bethune founded the National Council of Negro Women to work for the rights and opportunities of black people, especially black women. That same year, President Franklin Roosevelt appointed her as special consultant to the National Youth Administration (NYA), whose purpose was to provide employment and job training for youth. Later, as director of the Negro Division of the NYA, she helped increase educational aid for black students.

Mary Bethune also used her influence to secure a $500,000 grant for a black housing project in Daytona and forced Johns Hopkins Hospital in Baltimore to hire black physicians.

Although Mrs. Bethune's main concerns were the elimination of racial prejudice, improved status of black women, and greater job and educational opportunities for black youth, she was interested in helping other persecuted groups as well. When Nazi Germany passed the Nuremberg Laws in 1935, legalizing and extending discrimination against Jews, Mrs. Bethune and the National Council of Negro Women petitioned President Franklin Roosevelt to take action on behalf of Jewish victims.

She was a personal friend of Theodore Roosevelt and an adviser to five other presidents: Calvin Coolidge, Herbert Hoover, Franklin Roosevelt, Harry Truman, and Dwight Eisenhower.

When she died at age eighty, her will read: "I leave you love.... I leave you hope.... I leave you a thirst for education.... I leave you a responsibility to our young people...." But Mary McLeod Behune left more than that. For thousands of black people, especially women and children, she left increased opportunity, dignity, and self-respect.

W. E. B. DuBois

Author, Editor,
Civil Rights Leader
1868-1963

"I believe in the Negro Race: in the beauty of its genius, the sweetness of its soul, and its strength in that meekness which shall yet inherit this turbulent earth." — W.E.B. DuBois

A suspicious police agent once asked W. E. B. DuBois just what the NAACP was fighting for. "For the enforcement of the Constitution of the United States," DuBois replied. He knew what he was talking about: he was one of the founders of the organization.

Born in Great Barrington, Massachusetts, William Edward Burghardt DuBois was of African, French, and Dutch ancestry. After graduating from high school at age fifteen, he entered Fisk University in Nashville, Tennessee. From there he went to Harvard University in Massachusetts, where he received a Ph.D. and wrote his first book *The Suppression of the Slave Trade*. After leaving Harvard, he became a professor of English, German, Latin, and Greek, first at Wilberforce University in Ohio and then at the University of Pennsylvania.

At the University of Pennsylvania he wrote *The Philadelphia Negro*. As a result of this work, he was invited to teach history and economics at Atlanta University in Georgia. There he also directed the Atlanta University Studies Program, which published thirteen important studies of black life.

Dr. DuBois also maintained a strong interest in African affairs. Beginning in 1900, he participated in a series of Pan African conferences, where he demanded independence, self-government, and an end to colonialism in African countries. It was at the first of these conferences in London that Dr. DuBois made his famous prediction: "The problem of the 20th century is the problem of the color line." He was referring not only to the ongoing struggle for blacks to obtain basic civil rights in the United States but also to the efforts that would last more than fifty years to overturn oppressive European colonial regimes throughout Africa and Asia.

In 1903 Dr. DuBois published the work for which he is best known, a book of essays called *The Souls of Black Folk*. According to James Weldon Johnson, this work "had a greater effect upon and within the black race in America than any other book published in this country since *Uncle Tom's Cabin*." *The Souls of Black Folk* went into twenty-eight editions and was published abroad.

Two years later, DuBois organized the Niagara Movement. Named for the place where the first meeting was held (near Niagara Falls), the Niagara Movement was set up to demand "full manhood rights" for black people and was the forerunner of the NAACP. The NAACP grew out of a conference held in 1909 by a group of black and white leaders protesting the lynching of blacks.

A year later, DuBois established *The Crisis*, the official magazine of the NAACP, and ran it for twenty-four years. Largely because of his writings in *The Crisis*, the NAACP grew rapidly. By 1916 it had sixty-seven branches and 9,000 members.

Dr. DuBois criticized Booker T. Washington, another well-known black leader, for his policy of publicly ignoring injustices towards blacks for the purpose of maintaining good relations with whites. While agreeing with Washington that blacks should work hard and strive to become economically successful, he felt that blacks also should fight to protect their constitutional rights.

DuBois felt that college-educated blacks like himself constituted what he called "The Talented Tenth" who should take the lead in helping the black race to advance. It was an idea that was accepted by many educated blacks at the time.

Leaving the NAACP in 1934, DuBois returned to Georgia, where he became chairman of the Department of Sociology at Atlanta University. There he remained until 1944, pursuing dozens of research projects and writing hundreds of articles and essays. He also published several books, among them the brilliant *Black Reconstruction in America*.

Frustrated by the U.S. government's inability to solve the problem of racial discrimination, DuBois embraced socialism. He became associated with the peace movement and, after World War II, advocated banning nuclear weapons. Because of these involvements, the U.S. government indicted him as a foreign agent in 1951. When he appeared before the judge at his arraignment, the eighty-two-year-old DuBois stated, "It is a sad commentary that we must enter a courtroom today to plead Not Guilty to something that cannot be a crime—advocating peace and friendship between the American people and the peoples of the world. . . . In a world which has barely emerged from the horrors of the Second World War, and which trembles on the brink of atomic catastrophe, can it be criminal to hope and work for peace?"

Certainly the government thought so, even though protests and statements supporting DuBois poured in from all over the world. But Judge James McGuire, a political conservative, did not think the same way, and the case was thrown out on November 20, 1951.

Many individuals and organizations turned away from DuBois after his indictment and refused to publish his writings or hire him as a speaker. The State Department would not allow him to travel outside the country until 1958, and his mail was tampered with. According to DuBois, "It was a bitter experience, and I bowed before the storm, but I did not break."

In 1961, at the age of ninety-three, DuBois joined the Communist

Party. Two years later, he gave up his U.S. citizenship and became a citizen of Ghana, where he died on August 27, 1963.

Although Dr. DuBois rejected the United States at the end of his life, his influence here endures. The NAACP, which he helped to establish and in whose development he played a major role, has been the leading civil rights organization in the United States for more than seventy-five years.

William Edward Burghardt DuBois is considered one of the most influential black intellectuals, political thinkers, and protest leaders of his time. As a gifted social scientist, scholar, writer, and advocate of human rights both at home and abroad, he set a standard of black leadership that few others have been able to achieve.

Original leaders of the Niagara Movement in a photograph, 1905

Robert Sengstacke Abbott

Newspaper Editor,
Civil Rights Activist
1870-1940

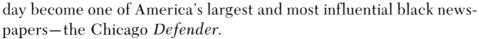

On May 6, 1905, Robert Sengstacke Abbott took all the money he had—twenty-five cents—and founded what would one day become one of America's largest and most influential black newspapers—the Chicago *Defender*.

Although he had graduated from Kent Law School, Robert Abbott was not successful in establishing a legal practice in Chicago. Fortunately, he had learned the printing trade at his stepfather's newspaper office in Georgia. Realizing he could better fight "segregation, discrimination, [and] disenfranchisement" publicly if he had more influence, Robert began his own newspaper. His office consisted of a chair and a card table in the kitchen of his landlady's rooming house. His first issue ran four pages, and he sold it door-to-door for two cents a copy.

Though the price was low, the time was right. White newspapers tended to ignore the black community except when reporting black crime. Advocating economic, social, and political justice usually was left to the few black papers that also provided an outlet for black ideas and writing.

During World War I, many blacks left the South in search of better jobs and greater freedom in the North. The Chicago *Defender* took the lead in encouraging this "Great Migration," much to the anger of some southern whites who feared the loss of cheap black labor.

Alarmed by the increasing number of lynchings, Robert Abbott printed the following militant slogan in the *Defender*: "If you must die, take at least one with you." The white community was outraged. Many southern towns outlawed the *Defender*. Copies of the paper had to be smuggled into black communities; some people caught reading it were beaten.

The *Defender* strongly supported the demands of the NAACP. In fact, each of them was listed in the masthead of the newspaper:

"First we want full manhood suffrage and we want it now. Second, we want discrimination in public accommodations to cease. Third, we claim the right of freemen to walk, talk and be with them that wish to be with us. Fourth, we want the laws enforced against rich as well as poor, against capitalist as well as laborer, against white and black. Fifth, we want our children educated. They have a right to know, to think, to aspire. We do not believe in violence. Our enemies, triumphant for the present, are fighting the stars in their courses. Justice and humanity must prevail. We are men, we will be treated as men. And we shall win."

In spite of his militant tone, Robert Abbott tried to ease tensions between the black and white communities. He served on the Chicago Commission of Race Relations and was active in the fight to break down segregated housing patterns. He backed political candidates who were sympathetic to black interests and fought to ensure that black workers were included in President Franklin Roosevelt's "New Deal" programs.

After years of effort, Abbott succeeded in making the Chicago *Defender* one of the most important black newspapers in the country. But it had been a hard, lonely fight. "My friends made fun of me," Abbott said. "They thought it was foolish of me to anticipate success in a field in which so many men before me had failed . . . but I went on fighting the opposition of my adversaries and the indifference of my friends; I emerged victorious."

Garrett A. Morgan

Inventor
1875-1963

On July 25, 1916, more than thirty men employed by the Cleveland Waterworks Company were at work in Tunnel No. 5, about 250 feet below Lake Erie. Suddenly, a violent explosion ripped through the area, trapping the men and filling the air with deadly gases. Rescue workers immediately arrived on the scene but the dense smoke prevented them from entering the tunnel. As the minutes passed, the chances of reaching the victims alive became more remote.

Suddenly, someone remembered that a man named Garrett Morgan had been demonstrating a new "breathing device" or gas mask, and they contacted him. Earlier, Morgan's invention had won a grand prize at a New York Safety and Sanitation Fair. No one had been too interested in his device then. But they were interested now!

As soon as Morgan was contacted, he and his brother, Frank, rushed to the tunnel entrance. Along with two other volunteers, they put on masks and entered the gas-filled tunnel. Feeling their way in the dark, they searched for the trapped workers. At the entrance to the tunnel, relatives and city officials waited. Would the gas masks work? Would their twenty-minute air supply be enough? What if there were another explosion?

Ten minutes later, Morgan and the volunteers appeared carrying the bodies of unconscious workers. Their work had just begun. Returning to the tunnel again and again, eventually, they brought thirty-two workers to safety.

Morgan's rescue mission made news nationwide. Suddenly, every fire department in the country wanted Garrett Morgan's gas mask. Orders poured in. Everyone was interested—until they found out that Garret Morgan was black. Then business declined. When Morgan promoted his invention in the South, he was forced to have a white man demonstrate how it worked while he pretended to be an Indian assistant.

Still, Morgan continued to perfect his device. In 1917 the United States entered World War I. Thousands of American soldiers used his gas mask to protect themselves from the enemy's deadly chlorine gas.

Garrett Morgan was born on a farm in Paris, Kentucky. He left home at fourteen and moved to Cincinnati, Ohio, where he got a job as a handyman. Because he'd had only six years of schooling, he hired a tutor to help him with his grammar. In 1895 he moved again—this time to Cleveland, where he got a job as a sewing machine adjuster. Before long, he had his own sewing machine repair business and, eventually, opened a tailor shop with thirty-two employees.

In 1913, while working with a polish for sewing machine needles, Morgan discovered a process that could straighten hair. Realizing the discovery could make him rich, he established the Morgan Hair Refining Company. He soon became wealthy. In fact, it is said that Morgan was the first black man in Cleveland to own his own car. The car led to another Morgan invention—the three-way traffic light. It was so successful that he sold the rights to the General Electric Company for $40,000.

Concerned about how poorly blacks were being treated, Morgan founded the *Cleveland Call* newspaper to improve coverage of black affairs. He also was an active member of the NAACP and, in 1931, ran unsuccessfully for Cleveland's City Council.

In 1963 Garrett Morgan, the man whose gas mask had meant the breath of life for thousands of people, died. He was eighty-eight.

William Christopher Handy

Musician, Composer
1873-1958

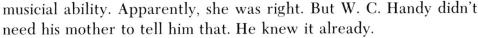

When William Christopher Handy was a young boy in Florence, Alabama, his mother told him that his big ears meant he had musicial ability. Apparently, she was right. But W. C. Handy didn't need his mother to tell him that. He knew it already.

As a child, William made music with harmonicas, broom handles, combs, earthenware jugs, even a nail that he used like a drumstick against the jawbone of a dead horse.

When he was older, he traveled across the country playing with small bands, trying to earn enough money to eat. Life was very hard on the road. Racial prejudice was widespread. Some say when William Handy wrote the words "I hate to see the evening sun go down," he was really thinking of his years on the road and of the many small towns where a strange black man was not welcome after dark.

W. C. Handy's first big hit was "Memphis Blues." It started merely as a campaign song for Edward "Boss" Crump, the mayor of Memphis. But its popularity soon gained wider appeal. Although Handy was cheated out of the profits on "Memphis Blues," he went on to write the even more famous "St. Louis Blues" in 1914 and "Beale Street Blues" in 1917.

When World War I created a labor shortage, many poor blacks left the South hoping to find better paying jobs in northern factories. Black newspapers, particularly the Chicago *Defender*, encouraged this trend, much to the anger of some southern whites who feared the loss of cheap black labor. As he traveled from town to town, Handy secretly distributed copies of the *Defender* to local black leaders. This was dangerous. More than one black man was lynched for distributing similar northern "propaganda."

During his travels, Handy began writing down the songs he heard. In 1918 he and his partner, Harry Pace, established the Pace and Handy Music Company. At that time, blues and jazz were becoming popular, and the company was a success. Many of W. C. Handy's compositions—"Aunt Hagar's Blues," "A Good Man Is Hard to Find," and "Careless Love"—became hits.

Prior to this time, blues was considered as the music of poor, ignorant blacks. Handy was determined to change this attitude. Even though he was troubled by serious eye problems and, in 1943, became blind, he continued to write and publish the music of black America. Long ignored by white musicians, blues music takes its rightful place today, in the forefront of American music, thanks to William Christopher Handy, the "Father of the Blues."

Henry Johnson

Soldier
1897-1929

On April 6, 1917, the United States entered World War I. Approximately 10,000 black men already had enlisted in the U.S. Army and thousands of others were soon signed up. Among the new recruits was a young man from Albany, New York, named Henry Johnson.

Johnson was sent to Camp Wadsworth, South Carolina, for training and assigned to the all-black 369th Infantry. Shortly afterwards, the 369th was shipped out to France, where it was attached to the Sixteenth Division of the French army and sent into action.

On the morning of May 14, 1917, Sergeant Henry Johnson and Private Needham Roberts were on guard duty on a bridge near the Aisne River. Suddenly, without warning, about thirty German soldiers attacked them. Cut off from the other American troops, Johnson and Roberts fought bravely. Wounded and out of ammunition, the two fought on in hand-to-hand combat. When the Germans took Roberts prisoner, Johnson, using only a knife and the butt of his empty rifle, freed him.

Finally, the Germans retreated, but only after Johnson and Roberts had killed at least four of them and wounded about ten others. Afterwards, Henry Johnson and Needham Roberts were taken to a French hospital. Johnson was treated for bayonet and grenade wounds to his back, arm, face, and feet.

The courageous stand he and Roberts had taken had prevented their regiment from suffering heavy casualties. The fight became known as "The Battle of Henry Johnson," and both men were awarded the croix de guerre, France's highest military honor.

The 369th Infantry was cited for bravery eleven times during the war. Germans called the black infantry unit "Hellfighters" because it never retreated and never allowed one of its members to be captured. But it paid a heavy price. In 191 days of fighting, the 369th suffered 1,500 dead and wounded. One hundred seventy-one of its officers and enlisted men received individual honors; the entire regiment received the croix de guerre for gallantry under fire.

When the war ended, the 369th was greeted with a tremendous parade up New York's Fifth Avenue. Henry Johnson received numerous promises of gifts and honors. But the gifts never materialized, and, although France had awarded him its highest military honor, he never received even a Purple Heart from the U.S. government. He also received no disability pay, even though he was incapacitated by his wounds and unable to work.

The courage and sacrifice of American black soldiers in World War I were little appreciated by either the U.S. military or the civilian population. Black soldiers continued to be segregated in the army and were discriminated against when they tried to find jobs after leaving the service.

President Woodrow Wilson had said that the purpose of World War I was to "Make the World Safe for Democracy." Thanks in part to the sacrifices of men like Henry Johnson, democracy remained safe in most European countries. Unfortunately, the struggle to make President Wilson's slogan a reality at home still continued to be fought.

Bessie Smith

Blues Singer
1894-1937

She once lost a job when she interrupted a song to yell, "Hold on. Let me spit!" That was Bessie Smith, later known to the world as the "Empress of the Blues."

Born in Chattanooga, Tennessee, in 1894, Bessie Smith was one of seven children. She grew up poor, and she grew up tough. Both her parents died when she was very young, so she was raised by her older sister Viola.

Bessie Smith loved music. When she was only nine years old, she began singing on street corners for nickels and dimes. It wasn't much, but it was a start. When she was eighteen, she got a job in a show where she met the great Gertrude "Ma" Rainey, a well-known blues singer who quickly spotted her talent.

For the next few years, Bessie traveled from town to town singing in clubs, tents, and theaters. It was a rough life. Often, singers had to work several shows a day in hot, crowded conditions, and theater owners didn't always pay what they had promised. Segregation was the rule throughout the South, and that meant travel was often difficult and uncomfortable. Once, a group of Ku Klux Klansmen showed up and began to cause trouble. Bessie Smith threatened them, saying, "You better pick up them sheets and run!" As she cursed them, they left in a hurry.

By 1920 Bessie Smith had become one of the most popular and highest paid blues singers in the country, attracting both black and white audiences. She worked with many of the best jazz musicians in the business, including Louis Armstrong, Charlie Green, James P. Johnson, Jack Teagarden, and Benny Goodman. Her singing influenced later artists such as Mahalia Jackson and Billie Holiday.

In 1923 she cut her first record, "Down Hearted Blues." It was an instant hit, selling more than two million copies. In fact, the success of her records kept Columbia Studios from going out of business.

Though she earned a lot of money, Bessie Smith never forgot the poverty of her early years. This is evident in the lyrics of her song "Poor Man's Blues:"

Mister rich man, rich man, open up your heart and mind,
Mister rich man, rich man, open up your heart and mind,
Give the poor man a chance, help stop these hard, hard
times.

For Bessie Smith the "hard times" got even harder when the depression of 1929 hit. Kind and generous, she had given a lot of her money away and had spent much of the rest. Although she was still able to work, the big money was no longer available. Radio was becoming popular, and, because of the depression, people weren't buying as many records. So Bessie Smith began touring the country again with a new show.

Things were going well for her until she was injured critically in an automobile accident near Clarksdale, Mississippi. She died in the Negro Hospital in Clarksdale a short time later. But her music continues to survive. When you listen to her songs, you'll understand why she is called "The Empress of the Blues."

Marcus Garvey

Orator, Black Nationalist
1887-1940

"Action, self-reliance, the vision of self and the future have been the only means by which the oppressed have seen and realized the light of their own freedom."
— Marcus Garvey

"We declare to the world that Africa must be free, that the Negro race must be emancipated." That was the message of Marcus Garvey. For millions of black people everywhere, he represented dignity and self-respect.

Born in St. Ann's Bay, Jamaica, Garvey was the youngest of eleven children. Although he was a good student, financial problems forced him to leave school at fourteen and become a printer's apprentice. After helping to organize a strike, Garvey was fired from his job. He worked briefly on a banana plantation in Costa Rica and for a newspaper in Panama and then went to London, England.

In London, Garvey worked for a publisher and studied nights at the University of London. There he met a number of Africans who involved him in their independence movement. When he returned to Jamaica in 1914 he organized the Universal Negro Improvement and Conservation Association and African Communities League (UNIA), with the intention of making Africa "the defender of Negroes the world over."

Intending to open a school in Jamaica similar to the one organized by Booker T. Washington in the United States, he accepted an invitation to visit Washington's school at Tuskegee, Alabama. When he arrived in the United States, however, he found that Booker T. Washington had died. Throughout the following years, Garvey toured the United States, speaking about the UNIA and the promise of a glorious black future in Africa. It was a message that attracted thousands of followers.

But Marcus Garvey did more than talk. In 1918 he began publishing the *Negro World*, which soon became one of the most popular black newspapers in the United States. He established the Black Star Line steamship company, the Negro Factories Corporation, the Black Cross Nurses, the African Legion, and the Black Eagle Flying Corps. Within two years, he had raised more than ten million dollars.

In August 1920, Garvey staged a month-long convention in Harlem, New York, featuring bands, receptions, rallies, and parades. Thousands attended from twenty-five countries and all forty-eight states. Before it ended, the delegates voted to create an African government with Marcus Garvey at its head and to organize the 400 million black people of the world into a free republic of Africa.

Unfortunately, before Garvey could realize any of his plans, his Black Star Line steamship company went bankrupt, and he was arrested for mail fraud in connection with the sale of Black Star stock. Convicted of the crime, fined $1,000, and ordered to serve a five-year jail sentence, Garvey entered Atlanta Penitentiary in 1925. Two years later, President Calvin Coolidge commuted his sentence but ordered him deported to Jamaica.

Marcus Garvey retired to London in 1935, where he died on June 10, 1940, following a stroke. His wonderful plans had failed; but he had captured the imagination of millions of black people as no other leader had before him.

Although his dream faded, Garvey's words remain sharp and clear: "Lose not courage, go forward . . . and you will compel the world to respect you."

Louis Armstrong

Musician, Singer, Composer
1900-1971

Louis Armstrong's musical career started with a bang when he was arrested for firing a pistol on New Year's Eve in 1913. The judge sent thirteen-year-old Louis to the Colored Waif's Home for Boys, where he learned to play the cornet. When he was released, he began playing in local jazz bands. Since he didn't earn enough money as a musician, he was forced to take additional jobs hauling coal, washing dishes, and collecting junk.

Poverty was nothing new to Louis Armstrong. He was born into a poor family in New Orleans on July 4, 1900. His parents separated shortly afterwards, leaving him to be raised by his grandmother until he was five or six years old.

He grew up in a section of the city famous for its bands and musicians. At nine, he was singing on street corners for pennies. After he learned to play the cornet, a musician named Joe "King" Oliver took an interest in him and began to help him with his technique.

At eighteen, Louis quit his other jobs and began playing the cornet full time. He even spent a year playing with an orchestra on a Mississippi riverboat. In 1922 King Oliver, who had left New Orleans several years earlier, convinced Louis to join him in Chicago. Within a few months, Louis was more popular than Oliver. After a nationwide tour with Oliver's band, people started calling Louis Armstrong one of the best musicians in the United States.

In 1924 he was invited to New York City to join Fletcher Henderson's band, which included some of the finest musicians in the country. While in New York, he switched from the cornet to the trumpet, the instrument for which he is best known.

When Armstrong returned to Chicago, he organized his own band: Louis Armstrong and the "Hot Five." Later, the band expanded and became the "Hot Seven." Many of their numbers became famous, such as "Gut Bucket Blues," "Heebie Jeebies," "Potato Head Blues," "Struttin with Some Barbecue," and "West End Blues."

Returning again to New York, Louis became a star in the musical *Hot Chocolates*. Later, he toured Europe, where he played for England's King George VI. He also toured Latin America and the Middle East. When he toured Africa in 1960, 100,000 people in Ghana came to hear him play. He was so popular that he became known as America's Ambassador of Goodwill.

Known for his rich, warm tones, inventive melodies, and powerful solos, Armstrong also became famous for his gruff singing voice and for "scat" singing—singing that uses meaningless syllables instead of words. Fondly nicknamed "Satchelmouth," or "Satchmo," Armstrong recorded numerous albums and made more than fifty movies.

When Louis Armstrong died in 1971, music lovers everywhere mourned his passing. The man who had been born on America's birthday had made a present of American jazz to the entire world.

Louis Armstrong and his early band, 1930s

Langston Hughes

Poet
1902-1967

The poem below, titled "Mother to Son," was written by Langston Hughes. The determination it expresses could apply to his own life. His father left home shortly after he was born. As a result, he spent much of his childhood with his grandmother, Mary Langston.

Mrs. Langston's first husband was Lewis Sheridan Leary, the abolitionist who had been killed while fighting with John Brown at Harpers Ferry. All she had to remember him by was the shawl that he was wearing when he died. Often, she would wrap herself in the blood-stained, bullet-riddled cloth and tell young Langston stories about the lives of Frederick Douglass, Harriet Tubman, and other freedom fighters. Sometimes at night, she would tenderly wrap the shawl around him as he slept. From these childhood memories came the strong black pride that later flowed through all of Langston Hughes's writing.

Mother to Son

Well, son, I'll tell you:
Life for me ain't been no crystal stair.
It's had tacks in it,
And splinters,
And boards torn up,
And places with no carpet on the floor—
Bare.
But all the time
I'se been a-climbing on,
And reachin' landin's,
And turnin' corners,
And sometimes goin' in the dark
Where there ain't been no light.
So boy, don't you turn back.
Don't you set down on the steps
'Cause you finds it's kinder hard.
Don't you fall now—
For I'se still goin', honey,
I'se still climbin',
And life for me ain't been no crystal stair. [4]

At thirteen, Langston was reading the poetry of Claude McKay, Carl Sandburg, and Walt Whitman. Following their example, he began to compose his own poetry. At nineteen, one of his poems, "The Negro Speaks of Rivers," was published in *The Crisis*, one of the most influential black magazines in the country. In it, he affirmed his link to his African heritage. Originally scribbled on the back of an old envelope, the poem was to become one of his most famous.

The same year, Hughes enrolled at Columbia University in New York City. Although he did well at Columbia, he was more interested in Harlem, where black music, theatre, art, and literature were flourishing during what was called the Negro Renaissance. Leaving college after only one year, he took several menial jobs and then signed on as a sailor on an old freighter.

Life on board ship suited Hughes and he responded by writing poem after poem. After traveling to Africa and Europe, he jumped ship and lived for a while in Paris, where he spent hours listening to the black musicians who had moved there to work. Once back in the United States, he continued to frequent the nightclubs, where black musicians performed, and to visit the storefront churches, where he was caught up in the marvelous rhythms of the sermons, spirituals, and hymns. He considered them "... like the waves of the sea coming one after another ... so is the undertow of black music with its rhythm that never betrays you, its strength like the beat of the human heart, its humor and its rooted power."

In 1924 Langston Hughes moved to Washington, D.C., where he got a job as a busboy at the Wardman Park Hotel. When he found that the poet Vachel Lindsay was staying at the Wardman, he arranged to show him some of his poems. Lindsay was so impressed that he read Hughes's poems to an audience that night. The response was overwhelming, and Hughes was invited to do his own reading.

His first book of poetry, *The Weary Blues*, was published in 1926. The same year he enrolled at Lincoln University near Philadelphia, graduating in 1929. While in school, he still found time to write poetry. Some black critics felt his second book, published in 1927, glorified immorality and showed blacks in a bad light. Hughes defended himself, saying, "I have a right to portray any side of Negro life I wish to . . . every 'ugly' poem I write is a protest against the ugliness it pictures."

Hughes's first novel, *Not Without Laughter*, was published in 1930. It portrayed everyday black life and was an immediate success. During this time, Hughes traveled widely and even spent a year in Russia. After returning home, he wrote a number of short stories that were collected in *The Ways of White Folks*, published in 1934.

Three years later, as a newspaper correspondent, he covered the Spanish civil war. When he returned home, he established the Harlem Suitcase Theatre. Its opening production—his own one-act play called "Don't You Want to Be Free?"—was a huge success. He later founded two other theatres—one in Los Angeles, the other in Chicago.

In 1934 Hughes began writing a regular column for the Chicago *Defender* in which he presented the shrewd, humorous views of a black man named Jesse B. Semple or "Simple." The Simple Stories, later collected into five books, are now considered to be among his best work.

In all of his writing, Langston Hughes celebrated ordinary black working people. He liked them, felt at ease with them, and respected them.

Hughes's work is notable for both its quality and its quantity. Over the years he wrote not only poetry but also plays, novels, children's books, short stories, articles, histories, biographies, radio and TV scripts, and his own autobiography. Known as the Poet Laureate of Harlem, Langston Hughes is primarily considered a poet. Often humorous, sometimes militant, occasionally subdued, his writing mirrored his observations, his beliefs, and, most of all, his hopes.

Frederick McKinley Jones

Inventor
1893-1961

When it comes to being cool, nobody can beat Frederick McKinley Jones, the man who put the freeze on the entire food industry and changed the eating habits of everyone in America. The whole thing came about when Jones overheard his boss, Joseph A. Numero, discussing the problem of developing an air-conditioner that would work in a truck.

Earlier truck refrigeration units took up too much space and tended to fall apart from vibrations caused by the movement of the truck on the road.

After much experimentation, Frederick Jones designed a small, light, shockproof refrigeration unit. But when he installed it under a truck, it became mud-clogged and broke down. His second unit, which he installed on top of the truck, worked just fine. Realizing the potential of his invention, Jones and his boss formed the U.S. Thermo Control Company, later called The Thermo King Corporation. Soon, they were manufacturing air-conditioners and refrigeration units for trucks, trains, airplanes, and ships.

Up until this time, many foods could be shipped only short distances before they spoiled. Thanks to Frederick Jones, fruit, vegetables, meat, and dairy products could be refrigerated and shipped all over the country. Refrigeration also made it possible to transport blood and medicines safely—a procedure that became very important during World War II.

But solving problems was nothing new to Frederick McKinley Jones. Born in 1893, in Cincinnati, Ohio, he was orphaned at age nine and sent to live with a Catholic priest in Kentucky.

In 1912 he moved to Hallock, Minnesota, where he got a job fixing farm machinery. When he wasn't working, he studied the fundamentals of electricity and mechanical engineering. After he returned from fighting in World War I, he began working with race cars and built the first radio station transmitter in Hallock and a soundtrack device for motion pictures.

It was at this time that Joseph Numero hired Frederick Jones to work for him, and it was the smartest move he ever made.

Frederick McKinley Jones received more than sixty patents for his inventions—forty for refrigeration alone. His work made it possible to transport food and medicines all over the world. Brilliant, creative, and hardworking, Frederick McKinley Jones was a cool guy in more ways than one.

Edward Kennedy "Duke" Ellington

Musician, Composer, Bandleader
1899-1974

"You go home expecting to go right to bed.... On the way, you [pass] the piano.... You sit down and try out a couple of chords.... When you look up it's 7 A.M." — Duke Ellington

At one time his mother had to force him to practice the piano. But by the time of his death at age seventy-five, Duke Ellington had become one of America's greatest composers. His musical legacy encompassed almost 6,000 pieces including more than 2,000 jazz compositions. He wrote musicals, concert pieces, scores for five motion pictures, a ballet, and religious music.

Born Edward Kennedy Ellington in Washington, D.C., he was nicknamed "Duke" because of the flashy way he liked to dress—always "duked out." As a boy, he was more interested in baseball and art than in music. In fact, when he finished high school, the Pratt Institute in New York City offered him an art scholarship. By that time, however, music had become more important to him.

Duke Ellington's interest in music began at the Poodle Dog Cafe, where he worked behind the soda fountain after school. The Poodle Dog had a small band and Duke Ellington was sometimes asked to sit in. At seventeen, he composed his first piece—"The Soda Fountain Rag." Not long afterwards, he began playing professionally. Sometimes his creativity led to trouble, however.

Once, Russell Wooding hired him to play one of five pianos in his orchestra. Four of the pianists played as they were supposed to—in unison. Ellington, however, decided the piece would sound better if he improvised. The audience loved it, but Mr. Wooding didn't. He told Ellington to improvise elsewhere, and fired him.

But Duke Ellington wasn't about to change his style. Instead, he formed his own band, "The Washingtonians." In 1922 they tried their luck in New York City. Ellington met several musicians there, including Willy "the Lion" Smith and Fats Waller, both of whom influenced his technique. But the trip was unsuccessful, and the band returned home. In 1923 they returned to New York and opened at the Hollywood Club at Forty-ninth Street and Broadway. Then in 1927, they played in Harlem's famous Cotton Club.

This marked a major turning point in Duke Ellington's career. The Cotton Club was the location of a regular radio broadcast. Before long, Ellington's theme song, "East St. Louis Toodle-Oo," was heard nationwide. In the five years he played the Cotton Club, he produced some of his most memorable music including, "Mood Indigo," "The Mooche," and "Rocking in Rhythm."

After leaving the Cotton Club, the Ellington band toured Europe and appeared in several movies. In spite of the pressures of the Great Depression and World War II, Duke Ellington continued to compose. Among the famous pieces he wrote at this time were "Solitude," "Sophisticated Lady," "Black, Brown and Beige," and "The A Train."

As his fame spread, Ellington was asked to perform at the Chicago Civic Opera House, San Francisco's Philharmonic Hall, and the New York Metropolitan Opera House.

Success never changed Duke Ellington. His first loyalty was always to his band and to his music. During the 1950s, when support for bands dropped off and many groups split up, Ellington insisted on keeping his band together. "It's a matter of whether you want to make music or make money," he said. "I like to keep a band so I can write and hear the music the next day.... A musical profit is more important than ... a financial loss."

Jesse Owens
Track-and-Field Athlete
1913-1980

Several years before World War II began, a twenty-two-year-old man named Jesse Owens handed Adolf Hitler a crushing defeat. The scene was the 1936 Olympics in Berlin, Germany. Jesse Owens, competing for the United States, had won four gold medals in the 100-and 200-meter events, broad jumps, and 400-meter relay. Hitler had long held that the Aryans were racially superior to blacks, Jews, and practically everyone else in the world. But Jesse Owens, in what was later called the most important sports event of the century, had proved him wrong.

Jesse Owens was born on September 12, 1913, in Danville, Alabama. He was the seventh of eleven children. Desperately poor, he began picking cotton in the fields at the age of seven. Back then, running was the farthest thing from his mind. After the family moved to Cleveland, Ohio, however, he began running track in high school. When he enrolled at Ohio State, he continued to run while he worked at several jobs to pay his tuition fees.

On May 25, 1935, Owens competed in the Big Ten College Track-and-Field Championships at Ann Arbor, Michigan. Within seventy minutes, he broke three world records and tied a fourth. People who watched him said, "It was one of those rare moments in sports when you can't believe what you are seeing," A reporter for the *Los Angeles Times* wrote, ". . . no one before or since has ever had a day like that and no one probably ever will." What made Jesse Owens's success even more amazing was that he competed while suffering from a painful back injury.

Owens's outstanding performance a year later at the Olympics made him one of the most famous athletes in sports history. When he returned from Germany, thousands of Americans greeted him with a ticker-tape parade. Although he enjoyed his celebrity status, Jesse Owens needed more than parades and cheers. His wife, whom he had married while still a teenager, was pregnant with their second child, and Jesse needed a job.

Unable to finish college because of lack of money, Owens took a job as a playground instructor earning $30 a week. When he was offered money to compete against a racehorse in a 100-yard dash, he accepted it. The money he earned from the race enabled him to return to college to get his degree.

Owens was offered other business ventures. He became part owner of a chain of cleaning stores. For awhile, the business was profitable. But when his partners disappeared in 1938, he was left with debts of $55,000. To pay them off, he took a job with the Ford Motor Company. "I buckled down,"he said, "and proved to myself that I had the talent to think as well as to run."

In 1949 the Owens family moved to Chicago, where Jesse went into the public relations business. Traveling extensively, he spoke to thousands of people about how athletic competition could improve racial problems and bring people together.

In 1976 President Gerald Ford awarded Jesse Owens the Medal of Freedom. Although he had set seven world records during his career, nothing was as meaningful to him as his Olympic victory. He often recalled:

"Ralph Metcalfe of Marquette University still was ahead of me at 70 meters, and 120,000 people were roaring. Between 70 and 90 meters, Ralph and I were streaking neck and neck. Then I was in front at the finish. My eyes blurred as I heard the "Star Spangled Banner" played, first faintly and then loudly, and then I saw the American flag slowly raised for my victory."[5]

Richard Wright

Novelist
1908-1960

"The impulse to dream was slowly beaten out of me by experience. Now It surged up again and I hungered for books, new ways of looking and seeing." — Richard Wright

When Richard Wright was four years old, he accidently set the house on fire. As punishment, he was beaten so badly that he lost consciousness and almost died. As he grew older, he suffered not from beatings but from poverty and hunger.

Hoping for a better life, the Wrights moved to Memphis, Tennessee, when Richard was very young. Shortly after they arrived there, Richard's father deserted the family. After he left, there was never enough to eat. At one point, things were so bad that Richard's mother placed him and his younger brother in an orphanage. Unhappy, he ran away but soon was caught and returned. Shortly after this incident, his mother took her two boys to live with relatives in Arkansas.

The murder of Richard's uncle and his mother's subsequent stroke forced the Wrights to move again. This time they moved to Jackson, Mississippi, to live with Richard's grandmother. The next few years were unhappy ones. Richard could not get along with his grandmother, and the family had very little to eat.

One encouraging thing about living in Jackson was that Richard was able to attend school regularly. Although his mother taught him to read, he had little formal schooling before the age of twelve. His love of reading and a vivid imagination convinced him that he would like to become a writer. In the segregated society in which he lived, however, such an ambitious goal seemed impossible for a poor black child to attain.

Discrimination and racial hostility tore at Richard's self-respect. He dreamed of saving enough money to leave Jackson. But the menial jobs he managed to get did little more than provide him with food money. One day in desperation, he stole a gun and some fruit preserves. With the money he made from selling them, he bought a ticket to Memphis.

In Memphis, Wright found work in an optical shop. Borrowing a library card from a friendly white man, he began reading whenever he could. Although he had gone no farther than the ninth grade in school, he soon became familiar with the writings of many of America's finest authors.

About 1927 Wright moved to Chicago, hoping to find greater freedom and opportunity. He worked as a dishwasher, porter, clerk, and insurance salesman. But when the depression crippled the U.S. economy in the 1930s, Wright, like thousands of others, found himself unemployed. Frustrated and miserable, he joined the Communist party, which promised racial justice. Later, he quit, believing that the Communists were using American blacks more than they were helping them.

Richard Wright's dream of becoming a writer began to come true after he moved to New York City in 1937. Within a year, a collection of his stories called *Uncle Tom's Children* was published. These stories reflected the prejudice and discrimination Wright had experienced while growing up in the South. Two years later, his most famous novel, *Native Son*, was published. It sold 200,000 copies in less than three weeks and established him as one of the country's leading authors. Unlike his earlier work, which portrayed the rural South, *Native Son* explored racism and oppression in the North as it affected a young black man named Bigger Thomas.

Following the success of *Native Son*, Wright completed a folk history called *Twelve Million Black Voices*. In 1945 he finished *Black Boy*, the story of his childhood and youth. Even more popular than *Native Son*, this book revealed the terrible poverty and racism that stunted the lives of most southern black children at that time.

Following his move to Paris in 1946, Wright became the leader of a group of writers, artists, and other intellectuals. He wrote *The Outsider* in 1953 and *The Long Dream* in 1958. In 1961, *Eight Men* was published, a book that includes his famous story "The Man Who Lived Underground."

Richard Wright is considered one of the finest authors this country has ever produced. His insights into American society shocked the public and exposed the terrible effects of racial prejudice.

Starved, beaten, and rejected as a child; forced to face unrelenting racial prejudice and discrimination as an adult, he made his way north and then overseas. He proceeded, he said,

"full of a hazy notion that life could be lived with dignity, that the personalities of others should not be violated, that men should be able to confront other men without fear or shame, and that if men were lucky in their living on earth they might win some redeeming meaning for their having struggled and suffered here beneath the stars."

A proud father, once a slave, poses with his children on their small southern farm.

Paul Robeson

Singer, Actor,
Political Activist
1898-1976

"We realize that our future lies chiefly in our own hands. We know that neither institution nor friends can make a race stand unless it has strength in its own foundation." — Paul Robeson

"An artist must elect to fight for freedom or for slavery. I have made my choice." It was a choice that would cost Paul Robeson his livelihood, but that would enable him to keep his self-respect.

The son of an escaped slave, Paul Robeson was born in Princeton, New Jersey, in 1898. When he was seventeen, he was admitted to Rutgers University. There he won twelve letters in baseball, basketball, and track and twice was named first black all-American in football. While still in his junior year, he was elected to Phi Beta Kappa, the national college honor society for outstanding students. He graduated in 1919 and was class valedictorian.

After graduation, he played professional football on weekends to support himself and enrolled at Columbia University Law School. He graduated in 1923, receiving his law degree in only two years. But by this time he had become more interested in acting.

When the famous playwright Eugene O'Neill saw him act, he asked him to play the lead in his play *All God's Chillun Got Wings*. Robeson's performance was well received. In 1924 he joined the cast of O'Neill's masterpiece, *The Emperor Jones*—again receiving critical acclaim.

By this time he also was becoming known as a singer. Although he had little training, his voice was rich and powerful. After hearing him sing, composer Jerome Kern gave him the part of "Joe" in the musical *Showboat*. The song "Ol' Man River" became the hit of the show. In later years, he often was asked to perform it at concerts and other occasions.

Paul Robeson's success in America was matched only by his success in Europe where audiences jammed concert halls to hear him perform. In 1930 he went to England to star in Shakespeare's *Othello*. It became his most spectacular triumph. "Dignified, magnificent and black—Paul Robeson . . . made stage history," said one critic. And when he toured the United States in the role, it was said, "There has never been and never will be a finer rendition of this particular tragedy. It is unbelievably magnificent. . . ."

In the late 1930s, Robeson became concerned with politics. He was active in the peace movement, in bettering labor conditions, and in obtaining racial justice. His strong beliefs led him to picket the White House, protest lynching, refuse to sing before segregated audiences, and sympathize with Communism.

As a result of his association with Communism, Robeson was called before congressional investigative committees and was blacklisted. Theater managers and stage and movie producers refused to hire him. The State Department revoked his passport, making it impossible for him to work overseas. His income, which in 1947 had been $104,000, dropped to $2,000 annually.

In 1958, however, a Supreme Court ruling in a related case forced the State Department to return his passport to him. Robeson tried to resume his acting and singing career but illness forced him to quit. He lived quietly in Harlem (later in Philadelphia) until his death in 1976.

Paul Robeson once said, "As I went out into life, one thing loomed above all else: I was my father's son, a Negro in America. That was the challenge." It was a challenge he was quick to meet.

Joe Louis

Athlete-Boxer
1914-1981

When he won, we all won— that's how black people felt about Joe Louis—and luckily, he won most of the time. Called the "Brown Bomber," Joe became heavyweight champion at age twenty-three and defended his title twenty-five times—more than any other boxer in history. In all, sixty-eight men went down before Louis's left jab and right hook.

Born in a tiny shack in Chamber County, Alabama, Joseph Louis Barrow was the fifth child of Lillie and Monroe Barrow. At age four, he was working with his mother in the cotton fields to help bring in money. Rarely able to attend school, he didn't begin to read and write until he was nine years old.

Meanwhile, his father died and his mother remarried. Her new husband, Pat Brooks, already had five children. He left them with Joe's mother while he went to Detroit, Michigan, to find work. Two years later, he sent for the family. They were still poor, but now they had an indoor toilet and electric lights—things they hadn't had before.

Joe began boxing when he was a teenager. In his first amateur bout, he was knocked down seven times in two rounds—not a very good beginning. But he made up for it. In his second bout, he won by a knockout. During his two years as an amateur light heavyweight, he won forty-eight of fifty-four fights by knockouts. About this time he dropped his last name, Barrow, and was known only as Joe Louis.

In 1934 Louis turned professional. His managers, John Roxborough and Julian Black, saw in him a future heavyweight champion of the world. They knew, however, that the battle to make him a champion would have to be fought outside the ring as well as inside it. White titleholders were sometimes reluctant to accept a challenge from a black contender, and riots often broke out when white boxers were defeated by blacks. Still, no one could ignore Joe Louis.

In 1935 he went up against Primo Carnera, the "Man Mountain," who stood six feet six inches and weighed 250 pounds. To prevent any trouble during the match, 1,300 policemen surrounded Yankee Stadium in New York where the bout was held. Three hundred undercover officers mingled with the crowd. Carnera went down in the eighth round, and the referee stopped the fight. Thousands of black people jammed the streets of Harlem to celebrate the win.

Then, in 1936 Louis was beaten by the German boxer, Max Schmeling. Adolf Hitler gloated, saying Louis's defeat proved that Germans were superior to blacks. For Joe Louis, it was a crushing defeat.

But he kept on fighting. In 1937 he won the heavyweight title when he defeated James Braddock. The win gave him a good feeling, but he was still bothered by his loss to Schmeling. On June 22, 1938, he met Schmeling in the ring again. This time, he won by a knockout in the first two minutes of the fight.

During World War II, Joe Louis's fighting career was put on hold while he spent four years in the army. A few years later, on March 1, 1949, he officially retired from boxing. He had successfully defended his title for eleven years and eight months—longer than any other man. In seventy-one professional bouts, he had been defeated only three times.

Loyal to his family and generous to his friends, Joe Louis was idolized by people across the country. For millions of black people who had little voice in society and who could not make themselves heard, Joe Louis's fists spoke for them.

Marian Anderson

Opera Singer
1902

"Everyone has a gift for something, even if the gift is that of being a good friend. Young people should try and set a goal for themselves, and see that everything they do has some relation to the ultimate attainment of that goal."—Marian Anderson

In 1939 Marian Anderson, one of the most famous opera singers in the world, was barred from singing in Constitution Hall in Washington, D.C. The reason? She was black. Constitution Hall was owned by the Daughters of the American Revolution (DAR). The organization, citing racial reasons, refused to let Miss Anderson perform there.

The incident made headlines across the country. Eleanor Roosevelt, wife of the president, resigned from the DAR in protest.

On Easter Sunday, 1939, Marian Anderson performed, instead, at the Lincoln Memorial in Washington, D.C. Seventy-five thousand people, including many diplomats and politicians, gathered to hear her. In response to the prejudice of the DAR, Miss Anderson sang "The Star-Spangled Banner," "America," "Ave Maria," and "My Soul Is Anchored in the Lord."

A quiet, dignified woman, Marian Anderson had always loved music. As a little girl, she often scrubbed her neighbor's steps to earn money to buy a violin.

She began her music career singing in a choir at the Union Baptist Church in Philadelphia, where she was born. Her wonderful contralto voice so impressed all who heard her that the congregation arranged for her to study with Giuseppe Boghetti, a world famous voice teacher. Soon Marian Anderson was singing professionally.

When she was twenty, she was given a chance to sing at Town Hall in New York City. But she was ill-prepared, and the concert went badly. Marian Anderson became so discouraged by this event that she came close to giving up singing. Yet, in 1925 she competed against other singers and won the Lewisohn Stadium Concert Award. Finally, her success led to a concert tour and an appearance as a soloist with the New York Philharmonic Orchestra. The opportunity for which she had trained so hard had arrived!

In the following years, Marian Anderson toured Europe, South America, Asia, and the United States. She sang to standing-room-only crowds in countries throughout the world.

In 1955 she became the first black person to sing at the New York Metropolitan Opera House. Two years later, at the request of the U.S. State Department, she toured twelve Asian nations. Upon her return in 1958, President Dwight D. Eisenhower honored her by making her a member of the United States delegation to the United Nations in New York City.

By the time she retired in 1965, Marian Anderson had received awards from the King of Sweden, the Emperor of Japan, and the President of the United States. She had sung at the inaugurations of presidents Dwight D. Eisenhower and John F. Kennedy.

The reaction of the music world to her talent can be summed up by the great orchestra conductor Arturo Toscanini. He said hers is the kind of voice that is "heard once in a hundred years."

Asa Philip Randolph

Union Organizer,
Civil Rights Leader
1889-1979

"The Negro should organize himself because with organization he will be better able to break down the barriers and prejudices of white workers against him than he will without . . . ." — A. P. Randolph

"Last hired, first fired." For millions of black workers, this was more than just an expression; it was a way of life, which included low pay and bad working conditions. Not until Asa Philip Randolph organized the Brotherhood of Sleeping Car Porters in 1925 did things begin to change.

Born in Crescent City, Florida, Asa Randolph spent his early teens working first in his father's small tailor and cleaning shop, and later, as a newsboy, grocery clerk, railroad worker, and driver. After completing high school at Cookman Institute, he enrolled at the City College of New York. There he worked at several poorly paid jobs while becoming concerned with the problems of black workers. He decided that the answer to many of these problems lay in unionization. But it was an answer that many employers did not like. They did not want unions—organizations to protect workers' rights. As a result, Randolph often found himself labeled a troublemaker and fired from his job.

During World War I, he tried but failed to organize the shipyard workers. Later, he was successful in organizing the Pullman railroad porters and maids. The formation of the Brotherhood of Sleeping Car Porters was only the first step, however. Over the next ten years, the union had a fight on its hands. The Pullman Company hired detectives to spy on workers and fired more than 500 people who were active in the union. After a long and bitter fight, Pullman finally agreed to recognize the union in 1937 and negotiated a new employee contract.

When the United States entered World War II in 1941, thousands of blacks volunteered for the service. Placed in segregated units, black soldiers faced many of the same discriminatory practices common during World War I. In the private sector, blacks were refused jobs in defense industries because of race. Determined to eliminate racial discrimination, Randolph threatened to lead a protest march on Washington, D.C., in July 1941. President Franklin Roosevelt called a conference of black leaders. As a result of this meeting, he issued Executive Order 8802, banning job discrimination in defense industries, and set up a committee on Fair Employment Practices.

Not until 1948 was the issue of discrimination in the armed services addressed. Then, President Harry Truman issued Executive Order 9981, stating, "There shall be equality of treatment and opportunity for all persons in the armed forces."

Throughout the 1950s, Randolph pressed for action against racial discrimination in labor organizations. In 1960 he established the Negro American Labor Council. Three years later, he organized and directed the famous 1963 march on Washington. It marked the highlight of his career, as over 250,000 marchers took to the streets to dramatize the need for civil rights legislation.

The demands that Asa Philip Randolph set forth for black workers were simple: equal opportunity, equal pay, and equal treatment. No one in the labor movement did more than he did to satisfy those demands.

Charles Richard Drew

Surgeon, Scientist, Educator
1904-1950

Thousands of U.S. soldiers lost their lives tragically in World War II. But thousands more stayed alive—even though gravely wounded—because of the medical research and dedication of Dr. Charles Richard Drew.

Born and raised in Washington, D.C., Charles Drew attended Amherst College, where he was an all-American football player. Following graduation, he took a job at Morgan College as a biology teacher and an athletics director.

Although Drew brought Morgan's basketball and football teams up to championship level, a medical career was what he really wanted. So he applied to McGill University Medical School in Montreal, Canada, and was accepted. While there, he became interested in the study of blood and how to preserve it.

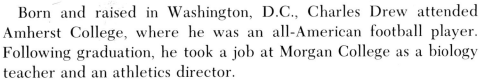

All people have one of four blood types: A, B, AB, or O. Should an injured person need a blood transfusion, it is important that the blood he receives be of his own type and that it "match" or be "compatible" with his own blood. In the 1930s, many patients died because not enough blood of the right type and match could be found quickly enough. The problem was further complicated by the fact that blood spoiled rapidly, making it very difficult to store.

Dr. Drew became fascinated with the problem of preserving blood. Shortly after graduating from McGill, he moved to New York to do graduate study at Columbia University and to work as a surgical resident at Presbyterian Hospital. While there, he performed numerous experiments on the physical, chemical, and biological changes that make blood unusable for transfusions. He learned that, while whole blood could not be stored longer than one week, blood plasma (the liquid portion of the blood without the blood cells) would keep much longer.

Meanwhile, the war raged in Europe. Nazi bombers were attacking England daily, and the number of casualties was mounting steadily. In August 1940, the "Blood for Britain" project was set up to make more blood available. But the program ran into serious trouble almost immediately. Different hospitals were using different standards for collecting and processing blood. As a result, much of the plasma reaching England was contaminated and had to be thrown out.

Black pilots of World War II

It was then that Dr. Drew received a cablegram from Dr. John Beattie, who was in charge of shock treatment and transfusions for the Royal Air Force in England. His emergency message asked Dr. Drew to ship 10,000 pints of plasma to him within one month. It seemed like an impossible task, but Dr. Drew did it. Soon afterward, he became the Medical Supervisor of the Blood for Britain program and standardized procedures for collecting, processing, storing, and shipping plasma.

Due to the success of his program, Drew was appointed as Red Cross director of a nationwide project to collect blood for the U.S. military. The project was going well until the armed forces told the Red Cross that it did not want any "colored" blood. Such a racist policy made no sense from any scientific or medical point of view. In an angry editorial, the Chicago *Defender* said.

No Negro blood accepted but—
When the terrible blitz raids of London . . . killed and wounded thousands . . . it was an American Negro surgeon [who organized] and [sent] U.S. blood plasma overseas.

No Negro blood accepted but—
When the Japanese bombed Pearl Harbor and maimed hundreds of American soldiers and sailors, it was blood collected by a Negro surgeon that saved their lives.[6]

Because of this kind of protest, the military agreed to accept "colored" blood but insisted that it be kept separate from blood donated by whites. To Dr. Drew this directive was completely unacceptable, and he resigned from the blood program.

On April 1, 1950, Dr. Charles Drew was killed in an automobile accident while on his way to a medical conference. Only a year earlier, he had been appointed surgical consultant for the U.S. Army European Theatre of Operations. The army, which had not wanted to accept his blood, had at least recognized the value of his advice.

Jackie Robinson

Major League
Baseball Player
1919-1972

"There are many of us who attain what we want and forget those who help us along the line. . . . We've got to remember that there are so many others to pull along the way. The further they go, the further we all go." — Jackie Robinson

I n 1962, in his very first year of eligibility, Jackie Robinson was elected to the Baseball Hall of Fame. Although he had tremendous athletic ability, he almost didn't make it to the major leagues.

At the time Jackie Robinson became active in baseball, the major league was open to white ballplayers only. Blacks competed in a separate Negro League. In spite of continuing pressure from the black press and various civil rights organizations, little headway had been made in changing the situation.

Born in Cairo, Georgia, in 1919, Jack Roosevelt Robinson learned at an early age that life would be hard. When he was only a year old, his father deserted the family. His mother then packed up her five children and moved to Pasadena, California, where she found work as a maid. After graduating from high school, Jackie attended Pasadena Junior College and later, UCLA. He became the first student to win letters in four different sports—baseball, basketball, football, and track. But during his third year at UCLA, he was forced to quit school and work to help support his family.

Soon after the Japanese bombed Pearl Harbor, Robinson was drafted into the army. Stationed at Fort Riley, Kansas, he was denied entrance to the Officers' Candidate School (OCS) because he was black. Robinson protested vehemently, both to the army brass and to world heavyweight champion Joe Louis, who was stationed at Fort Riley also. Louis used his influence with the War Department, and the military command at the base changed its policies.

After the war, Robinson signed a contract to play baseball for a black team called the Kansas City Monarchs. Meanwhile, Branch Rickey, president and general manager of the Brooklyn Dodgers, decided to integrate major league baseball. Moving secretly so as not to arouse opposition, he sent scouts to check out the Negro League teams and to report back on outstanding players. Jackie Robinson's name kept coming up on the scouting reports.

On August 28, 1945, Branch Rickey and Jackie Robinson met. Rickey wanted to sign Robinson to the Dodgers, but first he had to know if he could take the heat. A fight, an ugly incident of any kind, even if he were not at fault, could wreck their plans and cause a setback in efforts to integrate major league baseball. Could Robinson ignore the insults, threats, and deliberately thrown bean balls? The answer was yes.

In the spring of 1946, Jackie Robinson began playing with the Montreal Royals, the Dodgers' top farm club, and then joined the Dodgers the following year. These were rough years. Not only opposing players but also some of his teammates joined forces to make his life miserable. Several got up a petition protesting his presence. The president of the Philadelphia Phillies said his team would not play the Dodgers as long as Robinson remained on the roster. The St. Louis Cardinals threatened a protest strike. In response, Ford Frick, president of the National League, told the Cardinals,

"If you do this, you will be suspended from the league . . . . I do not care if half the league strikes. Those who do it will encounter quick retribution. They will be suspended, and I don't care if it wrecks the National League for five years. This is the United States of America, and one citizen has as much right to play as another. The National League will go down the line with Robinson whatever the consequence."[7]

The Dodgers, with Robinson's help, won the National League pennant that year. On September 30, 1947, Robinson became the first black to compete in the World Series (the Yankees won). He also was named Rookie of the Year. In 1949 he led the league with a .342 average and won the Most Valuable Player Award.

In 1957 Jackie Robinson was traded to the Giants but retired a month later. His success with the Dodgers had opened the way for other black ballplayers to enter the major leagues. Segregation in baseball had struck out!

Percy Lavon Julian

Chemist
1899-1975

Although his discoveries saved thousands of people from blindness, many scientists were never able to see beyond the fact that Dr. Percy Lavon Julian was a black man.

Born in Montgomery, Alabama, in 1899, Percy Julian struggled to obtain an education. Although he was accepted at DePauw University in Indiana, his high school education had been so inadequate that he was forced to take remedial courses along with his regular college courses. Nevertheless, he graduated with honors and was valedictorian of his class.

Percy Julian wanted to continue his education, but racial prejudice kept him from being accepted at leading graduate schools. So he took a job at Fisk University teaching chemistry. Two years later, when he was accepted at Harvard University, he continued his studies in chemistry. After graduation, he taught at West Virginia State College and, later, at Howard University in Washington, D.C.

From there, Percy Julian traveled to Vienna, Austria, where he studied for his doctoral degree and became interested in the medical uses of soybeans. After returning to the United States, he created synthetic *physostigmine*, a drug used to treat glaucoma, a disease that results in blindness. When Dean Blanchard, Julian's professor from DePauw University, heard of the discovery, he asked to have Julian appointed head of DePauw's chemistry department. But in spite of his qualifications, Julian was rejected—again for racial reasons.

If the medical and educational communities were making race an issue, W. J. O'Brien of the Glidden Paint Company was not. He hired Dr. Julian as chief chemist and director of research at Glidden. It was a smart move. Percy Julian's research allowed Glidden to go from a $35,000 loss to a profit of $135,000 in just one year.

During his lifetime, Julian owned more than 100 chemical patents. He developed "Aero-Foam," a substance that put out gas and oil fires and saved thousands of lives during World War II. His research on soybeans resulted in the manufacture of a synthetic hormone used in the treatment of cancer. He also developed a method of manufacturing *cortisone*, a drug that relieves arthritis pain.

In 1953 Dr. Julian founded Julian Laboratories, a pharmaceutical company. The first year his company made a mere $71.70. The second year he made $97,000. Six years later, he sold the company for $2,338,000.

As his scientific discoveries mounted, Dr. Julian was honored with numerous awards and citations. His medical and scientific achievements were responsible for saving thousands of lives and reducing the suffering of millions of people, including some who had tried to keep him from accomplishing anything at all.

Dr. Julian receiving an honorary degree of doctor of science from DePauw University, 1947

Ralph Bunche
Diplomat, Statesman
1904-1971

In 1950 the Nobel Peace Prize was awarded to an individual who temporarily brought an end to the bitter conflict between Jews and Arabs in the Middle East. The man who received the award was not an Arab or a Jew but a black American named Ralph Bunche.

Born in Detroit, Michigan, in 1904, Ralph Bunche and his family moved to Albuquerque, New Mexico, in 1914. Three years later, his parents died, and his grandmother took young Ralph and his sister to Los Angeles. There he finished high school and enrolled at UCLA.

After graduating with highest honors, Bunche enrolled at Harvard University in Cambridge, Massachusetts, where he earned a masters degree in government. While there, he met Dr. Percy Julian, the great chemist. Because of Julian's influence, Bunche was offered a teaching position in the political science department at Howard University in Washington, D.C. He accepted it and went to work enthusiastically. But he soon became discouraged by the segregation he found in Washington and returned to Harvard to get a Ph.D.

In 1936 Bunche published *A World View of Race*, in which he stated that racial prejudice exists partly because of economic needs. He wrote, "The Negro was enslaved not because of his race but because there were very definite economic considerations which his enslavement served. The New World demanded his labor power. . . . But his race was soon used [as the reason for] the inhuman institution of slavery."

In 1944 Dr. Bunche went to work for the U.S. State Department, becoming the first black acting chief of the Division of Dependent Area Affairs. At the close of World War II, he was involved in establishing the United Nations (UN). In 1946 he joined the UN as director of the Division of Trusteeship and Non-Self-Governing Territories. This section worked to protect the rights of people still under colonial control. It became an area of great concern after the war as many nations in Africa, Asia, and the Middle East strove to become independent of European rule.

In 1950 Dr. Bunche received the Nobel Peace Prize for having brought about a truce between warring Jews and Arabs in Israel. Although fighting in the Middle East would break out again in the future, the truce was a major accomplishment. Not only did it bring temporary peace to the area but it also showed that the newly created United Nations was capable of acting firmly to end the conflict.

In 1960 Belgium withdrew its control over the Congo (now called Zaire). Immediately, fighting broke out between different groups. Dr. Bunche was sent to bring peace to the area. His actions helped prevent a major war in central Africa and gave the new government a chance to survive.

During the next few years, Dr. Bunche continued his diplomatic activities, working to end fighting on the island of Cyprus, supervising peacekeeping troops at Egypt's Suez Canal, and serving as a mediator in a dispute between India and Pakistan. In 1968 he became undersecretary general of the UN, the highest rank ever held by an American.

In a statement that explained much of his success, Ralph Bunche once said, "I have a deep-seated bias against hate and intolerance. I have a bias against racial and religious bigotry. I have a bias against war; a bias for peace. I have a bias which leads me to believe in the essential goodness of my fellow man; which leads me to believe that no problem of human relations is ever insoluble."

Wilma Rudolph

Athlete, Teacher, Coach
1940

"To this day, black women athletes are on the bottom of the ladder. White women [athletes]... make it on the front cover of magazines. The Wilma Rudolphs don't. That's my challenge." — Wilma Rudolph

In 1960 the title of "World's Fastest Woman" was awarded to a young twenty-year-old who at age four was told that she might never walk again.

Born in St. Bethlehem, Tennessee, Wilma Rudolph was the seventeenth of nineteen children. Weighing only a slight four-and-a-half pounds at birth, Wilma struggled to survive as one illness after another kept her weak and bedridden. Then at age four, she was crippled by polio. Doctors said she would never walk again.

But Wilma's parents refused to accept her disability. They devoted their time and what little money they earned as a store clerk and a maid to help their daughter. The entire family took turns massaging and exercising Wilma's leg. Each week, Mrs. Rudolph would take her to a clinic ninety miles away for heat and water treatments. After a year of therapy, there was some improvement.

By the time Wilma Rudolph was eight, she was walking with a leg brace. A short time later, she was fitted with a special high-topped shoe that enabled her to get along well enough to go to school. Although she walked with a limp, she never allowed her disability to hold her back. She played basketball with her brothers in the backyard. Often, she played by herself long after they had quit for the day.

Wilma amazed everyone. One day, when she was eleven, she began playing basketball in her bare feet. Purposely, she had tossed aside her special shoe, confident that she could walk like everyone else. Within a few years, she was not only walking but also running—and running faster than many kids her own age.

By the time she was fifteen, she had become an all-state high school basketball champion. In her sophomore year, she broke the girl's state basketball record, scoring 803 points in twenty-five games. And her track-and-field record was even more remarkable.

In her final year of high school, Wilma Rudolph qualified for the 1956 Olympics to be held in Melbourne, Australia. There she competed as a member of the U.S. 400-meter relay team and returned home with a bronze medal. The next year, she attended Tennessee State, where she excelled in track. In 1960 she qualified for the summer Olympics in Rome and became the first American woman to win three gold medals in track—for the 100-meter dash, the 200-meter dash, and the 400-meter relay. As a result, she was voted U.S. Female Athlete-of-the-Year by the Associated Press.

After graduating from college, Wilma Rudolph married and became a teacher. Eventually, she expanded her career to include jobs as TV host, speaker, and coach. Her determination and perseverance allowed her to accomplish what no other American female athlete had been able to do.

The little girl doctors said would never be able to walk ended up running off with three Olympic gold medals and the admiration of the entire world.

Daniel "Chappie" James, Jr.

Pilot, Four-Star General
1920-1978

In 1945 Daniel "Chappie" James, Jr., then an air force lieutenant, took part in a civil rights action that got him arrested and almost court-martialed. Thirty years later, in 1975, he became the first black four-star general in the history of the U.S. military. In between, he flew more than 160 combat missions, stood up to Colonel Muammar Qadhafi of Libya, and commanded one of the most important centers of America's nuclear defense network at Peterson Air Force Base in Colorado.

Born in Pensacola, Florida, Chappie James was the youngest of seventeen children. His father was a foreman at the municipal gas plant, and his mother ran a school for black children. While attending his mother's school, Chappie James learned an important lesson, an "Eleventh Commandment"—"Thou shalt never quit." This lesson would remain with him all his life.

In 1937 he entered Tuskegee Institute in Alabama, where he became a popular campus leader. Two months before he was to graduate, he was expelled for fighting with another student. Tuskegee had strict rules of conduct, and not even Chappie James could get away with breaking them.

Having already learned to fly an airplane while in high school, Chappie James applied for admission in the Army Air Corps advanced flying program at Tuskegee. This program had been set up to prove that blacks were capable of piloting aircraft in combat. Standards for entrance to the program were high, and standards for graduation were even higher.

Chappie James was commissioned a second lieutenant in the Army Air Corps in July 1943 and assigned to the all-black 477th Bombardment Group at Selfridge Field near Detroit. In spite of Army Regulation 210-10, which states that all clubs and other facilities were to be open to all officers on duty, segregation persisted. Black officers were not allowed in clubs on base and were frequently denied promotions.

In an attempt to end increasing racial tension, the 477th was transferred to Freeman Field in Indiana. When black officers found the same discriminatory practices there, several staged a nonviolent sit-in at a segregated officers' club. They were arrested and charged with mutiny. Chappie James and more than 100 other black officers protested. They, too, were arrested and threatened with court-martial. Among the black officers involved with Chappie James were William T. Coleman, who would later serve as secretary of transportation in the Ford Administration, and Coleman Young, who would one day be mayor of Detroit. Eventually, General George C. Marshall ordered the charges against the black officers dropped and the regulation enforced. On July 26, 1948, President Truman ended segregation in the armed forces when he issued Executive Order 9981. Within a year, the air force had integrated its personnel.

Later, Chappie James was assigned to the Eighteenth Fighter Group at Clark Air Force Base in the Philippines, where he was seriously injured while rescuing a fellow pilot who had crashed. When he recovered, he joined his unit in Korea, where he won the Distinguished Flying Cross. Following his stay in Korea, he was named deputy commander at the Royal Air Force Base at Bentwaters, England, and later vice-wing commander in Vietnam.

In 1969 he was placed in command of Wheelus Air Force Base in Libya, where he confronted Colonel Muammar Qadhafi, leader of Libya. Qadhafi wanted the United States to leave the base in spite of a lease allowing it to stay until 1970. On October 18, Libyan troops under Qadhafi's command ran a column of halftracks (light armored vehicles) through the base. According to Colonel James, "I shut the barrier down at the gate and met Qadhafi a few yards outside it. He had a fancy gun and holster and kept his hand on it. I had my .45 in my belt. I told him to move his hand away. If he had pulled that gun, he never would have cleared his holster. They never sent anymore halftracks."

Colonel James remained at Wheelus until the base was closed. He then was assigned to the Pentagon and promoted to brigadier general in 1970. Five years later he was made a four-star general after being named commander in chief of the North American Air Defense Command (NORAD). It was a fitting climax in the military career of the first black four-star general in the history of the U.S. military.

NORAD protects Canada and the United States from enemy air attack.

Lorraine Hansberry

Playwright
1930-1965

"And because we are also, strangely enough under the circumstances, patriotic Americans, most of us...are still willing, despite the dogs and the hoses and the police, to set forth the message of our discontent by walking and talking."
— Lorraine Hansberry

When Lorraine Hansberry was twenty-six years old, she became the first black woman to have a play produced on Broadway and the youngest person to win the New York Drama Critics Circle Award for Best Play. Titled *A Raisin in the Sun*, the play was about the members of a black Chicago family and their efforts to move into an all-white neighborhood. This was a problem with which Lorraine Hansberry was familiar.

When she was eight years old, her own father, a hardworking, successful, Chicago businessman, moved their family into an all-white neighborhood. The reaction of the new neighbors was hostile. The Hansberrys were threatened, harassed, and finally evicted by court order. Mr. Hansberry, however, would not give up. With the help of lawyers from the NAACP, he challenged the lower court decision. Finally, in 1940, the U.S. Supreme Court ruled in his favor.

Meanwhile, Lorraine Hansberry had become interested in the work of black authors, particularly Langston Hughes. Graduating from high school in 1948, she enrolled at the University of Wisconsin, where she studied art and stage design. After completing her sophomore year, she moved to New York, where she met and married Robert Nemiroff, a music publisher.

During the next three years, Hansberry wrote her famous play *A Raisin in the Sun*. It was a wonderful play, but she had trouble getting it produced. Many producers felt there would be no interest in a serious black-oriented play. Besides, Lorraine Hansberry was an unknown black woman—three strikes against her.

Determined to see her play performed on the stage, she set out to find investors. Eventually, she found people willing to take a chance. *A Raisin in the Sun* was an immediate hit. Booked into Broadway's Ethel Barrymore Theater on March 11, 1959, it ran for nineteen months and was made into a movie that won the Cannes Film Festival Award in 1961. A musical version won the Tony Award in 1974, and the play itself has been translated into thirty languages around the world.

The success of *A Raisin in the Sun* made Lorraine Hansberry a celebrity. Because of it she was asked to comment on major political issues, especially as they related to women's rights and the growing civil rights movement. In 1964 she wrote the text for a book called *The Movement*, a collection of photographs documenting the civil rights movement. Her second play, *The Sign in Sidney Brustein's Window*, also opened that year.

In 1963 Lorraine Hansberry was diagnosed as having cancer, and it became increasingly difficult for her to write. She was in and out of hospitals until she died on January 12, 1965.

Fragments from her plays, letters, and stories were collected by Robert Nemiroff and made into a play called *To Be Young, Gifted and Black*. In it, Lorraine Hansberry's strength, pride, humor, kindness, and love of life shine through. "I wish to live," she wrote, "because life has within it that which is good, that which is beautiful and that which is love. . . . Moreover, because this is so, I wish others to live for generations and generations and generations and generations."

James Baldwin
Playwright
1924-1987

"I must oppose any attempt that Negroes may make to do to others what has been done to them. . . . I know the spiritual wasteland to which that road leads. . . ."—J. Baldwin

"And God gave Noah the rainbow sign. No more water, the fire next time!" These lines from an old Negro spiritual gave James Baldwin the title for one of his most famous books, *The Fire Next Time*. That Baldwin should draw on a religious song for inspiration is not surprising, since he began preaching at age fourteen.

In turning to the church, young James was following the example of his father, the Reverend David Baldwin. Yet, James and his father were usually in conflict.

Born in New York City's Harlem in 1924, James was small and somewhat "frogeyed." Other children often teased him about his looks. Feeling unloved and ugly, he would spend hours by himself in the public library reading and writing plays, poetry, and short stories.

In 1938 Baldwin entered DeWitt Clinton High School in the Bronx, New York, where he became editor of the school newspaper. For the first time, he found friends who also enjoyed reading and writing. But his new friends were white and Jewish—people his father did not approve of and would not allow in his house.

Resentful of his father and unable to cope with mounting family problems, James Baldwin left home at age seventeen and began working on his first novel *Go Tell It on the Mountain*.

In 1944 he met Richard Wright, the famous black novelist. With his help, he obtained a Eugene Saxon Memorial Trust Award, which enabled him to continue his writing. In 1948 his first short story, "Previous Condition," was published, although he still had not been able to complete his novel.

Feeling torn between his loyalty to the black community that laughed at his dreams of becoming a writer and his white friends who could not understand the tension he felt as a black man living in a racist society, Baldwin moved to Paris.

Soon, money became a major problem. Hungry and broke, Baldwin was forced to sell some of his clothes and even his typewriter. However, living in France provided a healthy environment for his writing. The French did not reject him because of his color. Nor did they sneer at his desire to write. This enabled him to do what he could not do in the states—creatively use his past and his black experience instead of trying to escape from them.

In 1949 his essay "Everybody's Protest Novel" was published. The publication of this essay, however, destroyed his friendship with Richard Wright. Suffering a nervous breakdown, Baldwin went to Switzerland to recover. There he finally completed his novel *Go Tell It on the Mountain*.

After living four years in Europe, he returned to the United States and sold his novel. A year later, he returned to Europe to work on a second book, *Another Country*, and a play called *The Amen Corner*. Unable to finish either of these to his satisfaction, he put both aside and wrote what would become his favorite novel, *Giovanni's Room*.

Becoming more and more preoccupied with the growing civil rights movement in America, Baldwin returned to the United States. There he began to take part in sit-ins and allowed his name to be used by the movement for raising money.

In 1955 the vicious murder in Mississippi of a fourteen-year-old black youth named Emmett Till had a strong impact on Baldwin; so did a trip he later took with civil rights leader Medgar Evers to investigate the murder of a black man by a white storekeeper. Later, these experiences became the driving force behind his play *Blues for Mister Charlie.*

As a result of books such as *Notes of a Native Son*, *Nobody Knows My Name*, and *The Fire Next Time*, James Baldwin became known as a novelist and an essayist. Angry, yet somehow hopeful, his essays, like his novels and plays, often focused on what he saw as the continuing, intertwining destinies of blacks and whites in America. ". . . [W]e, the black and white, deeply need each other here if we are really to become a nation," he wrote, ". . . if we are really, that is, to achieve our identity, our maturity, as men and women."

Rosa Parks
Civil Rights Activist
1913

"I'm just an average citizen. Many black people before me were arrested for defying the bus laws. They prepared the way."
— Rosa Parks

Shortly after 5:00 P.M. on Thursday, December 1, 1955, Rosa Parks finished her work as a seamstress at a local department store in Montgomery, Alabama, and boarded a bus. What began as an ordinary bus ride home became, instead, the event that sparked the civil rights movement of the 1960s.

Rosa McCauley Parks was born in Tuskegee, Alabama, in 1913 and grew up on a small farm with her brother, mother, and grandparents. She attended an all-black school that closed three months earlier than white schools so that the children could work in the fields.

When Rosa turned eleven, her mother had saved enough money to send her to a private school in Montgomery. She attended high school until her mother became ill. After quitting school, she found a job as a house servant and began sending money back to her family in Tuskegee. When Rosa married Raymond Parks, she returned to high school and graduated.

In 1943 she joined the NAACP and worked to ensure voting rights for blacks. She continued to work for the NAACP while she held various jobs as housecleaner, seamstress, and office clerk.

One December evening in 1955, while returning home from work, Mrs. Parks boarded a bus and sat down. According to Montgomery law, blacks were required to sit in the back of the bus and to give up their seats to white passengers as the bus filled up. When Mrs. Parks was asked to give up her seat to a white passenger on this particular evening, however, she refused. Immediately, the driver stopped the bus and called two policemen. Mrs. Parks was arrested and taken to jail for violating the city ordinance.

Edgar Daniel Nixon, head of the NAACP in Montgomery, posted a $100 bond to get her released. He then called a meeting of black leaders to determine what action they should take. Although Mrs. Parks was not the first black person to be arrested for refusing to give up her seat on a bus, E. D. Nixon decided that she would be the last.

The meeting was held in the basement of the Dexter Avenue Baptist Church, where a young man named Martin Luther King, Jr., had just been appointed minister. By the end of the long evening the leaders agreed to call a one-day boycott of all city buses for Monday, December 5.

Over the weekend, thousands of leaflets announcing the boycott were printed and distributed. On Monday morning, the first buses began their run through the black neighborhoods. They finished the same way they had begun—empty. There were no black passengers. The boycott was a success. Immediately, organizers voted to continue it. They set up the Montgomery Improvement Association (MIA) and named Martin Luther King, Jr., its leader.

Meanwhile, Rosa Parks went to court. She was charged with violating a 1947 segregation statute. The judge found her guilty and fined her $10 plus $4 in court costs. But the NAACP appealed the case to the U.S. Supreme Court.

While the boycott continued, the Ku Klux Klan and the White Citizens Council took action. They threatened the MIA organizers and harassed blacks on the street. Hundreds of leaders and supporters, including Rosa Parks, were arrested. They all lost their jobs. Dr. King's house was dynamited. Still the boycott continued.

Black people walked. They rode bicycles, caught cabs, and joined car pools. They drove wagons, hitchhiked, rode mules, and then walked some more. One elderly woman responded, "My feets is tired, but my soul is rested."

After 381 days of boycotting, the U.S. Supreme Court ruled in favor of Rosa Parks. It declared Alabama laws on bus segregation unconstitutional. In April 1956, the bus company, which had lost more than $750,000 during the long boycott, agreed to integrate seating on its buses and to hire black drivers. And with that, segregation on Montgomery, Alabama, buses rolled to a dead stop!

Thurgood Marshall

U.S. Supreme Court Justice
1908

The U.S. Supreme Court stands at First and East Capital Streets, N.E., in Washington, D.C. Etched into the stone over its entrance are the words "Equal Justice Under Law." For many years, those words were only scratches on a wall as far as black people were concerned. But to Thurgood Marshall, the man who would one day become the first black Supreme Court justice, they were a promise and a commitment.

Thurgood Marshall was born in Baltimore in 1908. The fact that his mother was a teacher did not keep him from frequently getting into trouble at school. As punishment, the principal would send him to the school basement to memorize sections of the U.S. Constitution. This didn't keep Thurgood out of trouble, but did help him later when he argued cases before the court.

After graduating with honors from Lincoln University in Pennsylvania, Thurgood Marshall went to Howard University Law School in Washington, D.C. Finishing in 1933, he entered private practice, specializing in civil rights cases. In 1936 he began working for the NAACP in Baltimore, becoming head of its legal staff in 1938.

One of the civil rights cases he accepted was that of Lloyd Lionel Gaines, a student who was seeking admission to the all-white University of Missouri Law School.

In 1896 the Supreme Court had ruled in the case of *Plessy* v. *Ferguson* that it was legal for a state government to maintain separate or segregated facilities for blacks and whites, provided the facilities were "equal." The "separate but equal" doctrine that was set forth in *Plessy* v. *Ferguson* originally referred to railroad cars, but later it included schools and other facilities.

Once a ruling has been handed down by the Supreme Court, it becomes very difficult to overturn. The reason is that people cannot be expected to know what the law is if the court keeps changing its mind. Therefore, once the Supreme Court has handed down a ruling, it establishes what is known as a "precedent." Later, when other cases arise on related issues, lawyers and judges can refer to the court's past rulings (precedents) on the subject to determine how the law should be interpreted.

In the *Gaines* case, Marshall did not attack segregation directly, but pointed out that "equal" did not exist in this situation. Because there was no separate law school for blacks at the University of Missouri, the Supreme Court ruled that the university would either have to admit Gaines or provide him with an opportunity to attend a comparable law school within the state. Although Gaines eventually entered law school at the University of Michigan, his case established an important precedent—that for segregation to be allowable it must be equal. The question then became—What is equal?

That issue came up in another Thurgood Marshall case—*Sweatt* v. *Painter* in 1950. Herman Sweatt had been denied entrance to the all-white University of Texas Law School in 1946. When he sued, the Texas courts gave the state six months to set up a separate black law school. But Marshall was able to persuade the U.S. Supreme Court that a hastily set up, makeshift law school could in no way provide an education equivalent to that provided by the university. As a result, the Court ordered Sweatt admitted.

By 1954 Marshall was ready to challenge school segregation. The case was *Brown* v. *The Board of Education of Topeka, Kansas*. Drawing partly on psychological studies, Marshall convinced the Court that segregated education could never result in equal education. Segregated black children concluded that they were not as good as white children. Segregation automatically implied inferiority, argued Marshall, and automatically placed black children at a disadvantage. The Court unanimously agreed.

Unfortunately, winning the case did not result in immediate school desegregation. The Supreme Court had ordered the states to integrate their schools "with all deliberate speed." In many areas, this meant no speed at all. Prince Edward County in Virginia completely closed its schools for five years rather than integrate them. Thurgood Marshall and his staff persisted, filing case after case to force individual school districts to obey the Supreme Court's ruling.

But school desegregation was not Thurgood Marshall's only concern. As chief counsel for the NAACP, and later as director-counsel for its Legal and Educational Fund, he directed and coordinated legal attacks on discrimination in voting, housing, restaurants and other public places, buses, and criminal procedure. He traveled thousands of miles interviewing witnesses, locating evidence, and arguing cases.

Of the thirty-two major cases he argued for the NAACP, Thurgood Marshall won twenty-nine. His record as judge of the U.S. Court of Appeals for the Second Circuit was equally impressive. Of the more than 150 opinions he handed down while judge in this court, none was ever reversed by a higher court. In 1965 President Lyndon Johnson appointed him solicitor general of the Department of Justice. Of the nineteen cases he argued for the government, he won fourteen.

When President Johnson appointed Thurgood Marshall associate justice of the Supreme Court in 1967, he became the first black man to serve in this position. It was a fitting climax in the career of a man who had done so much to translate the words "Equal Justice Under Law" into reality.

On June 27, 1991, eighty-two-year-old Marshall resigned from the Supreme Court due to failing health. His contributions have changed America.

The Little Rock Nine

On the morning of September 4, 1957, fifteen-year-old Elizabeth Eckford arrived at school and was met by a National Guardsman armed with a bayonet. She turned around and, with a taunting mob at her heels, walked 100 yards, alone, to a bus stop. The school year at Central High School in Little Rock, Arkansas, had begun.*

Three years earlier, in 1954, the U.S. Supreme Court had ruled in a case called *Brown* v. *The Board of Education* that black and white children must be allowed to attend school together. The court had overturned earlier rulings that had permitted the segregation of black and white children, provided the schools they attended were "separate but equal." Thurgood Marshall, a lawyer for the NAACP, had presented the legal argument for Brown, pointing out that the schools were not equal. They lacked adequate money, books, and basic materials and were often in poor physical condition. He argued further that a school board's insistence that black children be kept away from white children was wrong and discriminatory in and of itself.

In September 1957, however, the NAACP decided to take action. It selected nine black students, one of whom was Elizabeth Eckford, from a group of over eighty applicants to integrate the school in Little Rock.

Several weeks after Elizabeth Eckford's experience, the nine students, armed with a federal court order, tried to attend classes. Four hours later, they were taken home as an unruly mob of 1,000 screaming segregationists roamed the streets outside the school. The next day, the nine stayed home. But on September 25, they finally attended classes under the protection of the U.S. Army's 101st Airborne Division.

For the rest of that year, the Little Rock Nine, as they had come to be called, attended class under military escort. They learned algebra, biology, English, and chemistry—but made history themselves.

*See pages 224-226 for Elizabeth Eckford's account of day one at Central High School.

Medgar Evers

Civil Rights Activist
1925-1963

"If I die, it will be in a good cause. I've been fighting for America just as much as the soldiers in Vietnam." — Medgar Evers

In 1955 his name topped a nine-man death list; but the list was shortened to eight when the Reverend George T. Lee was gunned down in Belzoni, Mississippi. Then, in 1963, Medgar Evers was killed too, shot in the back as he returned home from a meeting. As far as the murderers were concerned, both Evers and Lee were guilty of the same crime: they wanted blacks to exercise their right to vote. This is what the killers were trying to prevent.

Born in Decatur, Mississippi, Medgar Evers was the third of four children. At one time he had to walk twelve miles each way to get to school, but Evers was determined to get an education. After his discharge from the army, he returned to Mississippi and enrolled at Alcorn A & M College. He graduated in 1952 and joined the NAACP. Because of his leadership abilities, Evers was appointed field secretary after only two years.

At that time, segregation in most public places was still in effect. Evers worked hard to end it. He made speeches, led demonstrations, and encouraged blacks to boycott stores owned by white businessmen who refused to hire or promote black workers. Although Evers knew his work was dangerous, he refused to quit.

When Medgar Evers was killed, demonstrations and rallies occurred nationwide, and black voter registrations increased. Pressured by the unrest, President John F. Kennedy requested passage of a new civil rights act outlawing racial segregation in public places.

Although some people said that voting was a waste of time, Medgar Evers knew better. Because of people like him, black men and women now hold political office, and segregation in public places is against the law in the United States.

Sit-Ins

"I sat-in at a restaurant for six months, and when they finally agreed to serve me, they didn't have what I wanted"—so went a famous line. In reality, the sit-in movement was no joke. It began in Greensboro, North Carolina, at 4:30 P.M. on the afternoon of February 1, 1960. On that day, Ezell Blair Jr., Joseph McNeil, David Richmond, and Franklin McClain entered an F. W. Woolworth store. They sat down at a segregated lunch counter, ordered coffee, and then refused to leave when told, "We don't serve Negroes."

The four young men had expected not to be served. What no one had expected, however, was that they would sit there and politely, but firmly, refuse to leave. This was 1960, and throughout the South black people were not allowed to sit at the same lunch counters with whites, swim at the same beaches, use the same water fountains, or worship at the same churches. Segregation was the law, and it meant separation of the races in every way.

The next day, the four returned to Woolworth's—this time accompanied by sixteen other students. Again they sat at the lunch counter and requested service. Again they were refused. And again, they declined to leave. On Wednesday, February 3, seventy students filled the Woolworth's store. This time, the group included white students as well as black. Many brought school books and studied while they waited. By this time, their protest had become known nationwide as a "sit-in."

On Thursday, there was trouble. An angry group of white teenagers began shoving and cursing them but were quickly removed by the police. By February 10, the sit-in movement had spread to five other states.

By September 1961, more than 70,000 people, both black and white, had participated in sit-ins at segregated restaurants and lunch counters, kneel-ins at segregated churches, read-ins at segregated libraries, and swim-ins at segregated pools and beaches. Over 3,600 people had been arrested, and more than 100 students had been expelled. But they were getting results. Many places did agree to integrate. On June 10, 1964, the U.S. Senate passed a major civil rights bill outlawing racial discrimination in all public places. President Lyndon Johnson signed it on July 2, and it became law. But the highest credit still goes to the four brave students from North Carolina who first sat-in and waited it out.

Students sitting at Woolworth's segregated lunch counter in Atlanta, Georgia

Freedom Riders

"I'm taking a trip on the Greyhound Bus line. I'm riding up front, into Jackson this time." Those were the lyrics, but the opening beat was provided by thirteen Freedom Riders (seven black and six white) who went on the road May 4, 1961, to desegregate southern bus terminals. An angry mob carrying chains and baseball bats met them in Anniston, Alabama, and firebombed their bus.

Although the U.S. Supreme Court had ruled in 1946 and 1960 that segregation was illegal on interstate buses, in much of the South segregation prevailed. At bus stations, blacks were forced to use separate waiting rooms, restrooms, and ticket counters. Black passengers were allowed to sit only in seats in the back of the buses. If all the seats in the back were taken, black riders had to stand, even if there were empty seats in the front. So the Congress of Racial Equality (CORE), a civil rights group under the direction of James Farmer, began the "Freedom Rides."

The first group of Freedom Riders traveled peacefully through Virginia and North Carolina. In South Carolina, two members of their party were attacked, but the group continued its journey. In Georgia, things were quiet. In Anniston, Alabama, a mob shot out the tires of one bus, broke a window, and tossed a firebomb inside. The bus went up in flames and the Freedom Riders barely got out alive. The second bus made it into Birmingham. There, Police Commissioner Eugene "Bull" Connor, a segregationist, told city police officers to take fifteen minutes to "visit their mothers" (it was Mother's Day) so Freedom Riders would be unprotected. The Riders were attacked by Ku Klux Klan thugs and beaten viciously. James Peck, a white CORE member, required fifty-six stitches after his head was bashed in with lead pipes.

After Anniston, CORE members were joined by young people from the Student Nonviolent Coordinating Committee (SNCC), another civil rights group. Together they rode into Montgomery, Alabama, where Dr. Martin Luther King was to address them at a mass rally at the First Baptist Church. Again rioters attacked, and, when the local police failed to protect the group, U.S. Attorney General Robert F. Kennedy sent in 600 U.S. marshals to restore order.

That night, 1,200 blacks gathered at the church. An angry mob showed up, but marshals stepped in, and it backed down. Meanwhile, Governor Patterson declared martial law and ordered the Alabama National Guard under General Henry Graham to the church. The governor called the attorney general and told him that General Graham couldn't guarantee Martin Luther King's safety. "Have the general call me," said Kennedy angrily. "I want him to say it to me. I want to hear a general of the U.S. Army say he can't protect Martin Luther King." Of course, General Graham had said no such thing, and the National Guard finally dispersed the mob and led Dr. King and the others to safety.

In the months that followed, there were more Freedom Rides and hundreds of arrests—350 in Jackson, Mississippi, alone. Hundreds were thrown in jail after being charged with disorderly conduct, disturbing the peace, and trespassing. Still, they kept coming. Finally, segregation on buses was brought to an end; but it had been a hard road to travel.

Freedom riders bus on fire outside Anniston, Alabama

Fannie Lou Hamer

Civil Rights Activist
1917-1977

"I'm sick and tired of being sick and tired."
— Fannie Lou Hamer

"You can pray until you faint, but if you don't get up and try to do something, God is not gonna put it in your lap." So spoke Fannie Lou Hamer at a mass meeting in Indianola, Mississippi, in August 1964. Her purpose was to encourage black people to register to vote. It was dangerous work. A year earlier, she had been beaten up for doing it.

Born October 6, 1917, in Mississippi, Fannie Lou Hamer was the youngest of twenty children. Her parents were sharecroppers. Sharecropping, or "halfing," as it is sometimes called, is a system of farming whereby workers like Fannie Lou Hamer and her family are allowed to live on a plantation in return for working the land. When the crop is harvested, they split the profits in half with the plantation owner. Sometimes the owner pays for the seed and fertilizer, but usually the sharecropper pays those expenses out of his half. It's a hard way to make a living, and sharecroppers generally are born poor, live poor, and die poor.

At age six, Fannie Lou began helping her parents in the cotton fields. By the time she was twelve, she was forced to drop out of school and work full time to help support her family. Once grown, she married another sharecropper named Perry "Pap" Hamer.

On August 31, 1962, Fannie Lou Hamer decided she had had enough of sharecropping. Leaving her house in Ruleville, she and seventeen others took a bus to the courthouse in Indianola to register to vote. On their return home, police stopped their bus. They said it was painted the wrong color. Hamer and the others were arrested and jailed.

After being released from jail, the plantation owner paid Fannie Hamer a visit. He told her that if she insisted on voting, she would

Sharecropping in the South

have to get off his land, even though she had lived there for eighteen years. Mrs. Hamer refused to back down and she was forced to leave the plantation that same day. (Her husband and two daughters were forced to leave later.) That evening, night riders fired sixteen bullets into the home of Mrs. Turner, the lady with whom she had gone to stay. Still, Mrs. Hamer would not give up. "We're tired of all this beating," she said. "We're tired of taking this. It's been a hundred years and we're still being beaten and shot at. Crosses are still being burned because we want to vote. But I'm going to stay in Mississippi, and if they shoot me down, I'll be buried here."

By this time, Mrs. Hamer had begun working on welfare and voter registration programs for two civil rights organizations—the Southern Christian Leadership Conference (SCLC) and SNCC.

In 1964 presidential elections were being held. In an effort to focus greater national attention on voting discrimination, civil rights groups created the Mississippi Freedom Democratic Party (MFDP). This new party sent a delegation, which included Mrs. Hamer, to Atlantic City, where the Democratic Party was holding its presidential convention. Its purpose was to challenge the regular all-white Mississippi delegation on the grounds that it didn't fairly represent all the people of Mississippi.

At the convention, a compromise was reached that gave voting and speaking rights to two delegates from the MFDP and seated the rest as honored guests. The Democrats agreed that in the future no delegation would be seated from a state where anyone was illegally denied the vote. A year later, President Johnson pushed a voting rights bill through Congress that protected black voters.

Fannie Lou Hamer continued to work on equal rights and anti-poverty programs in later years. In speaking of prejudice and discrimination, she once said, "This ain't just Mississippi's problem. It's America's problem." But thanks to people like Fannie Lou Hamer, it's less of a problem today.

Malcolm X

Civil Rights Leader
1925-1965

"We have to keep in mind at all times that we are not fighting for integration, nor are we fighting for separation. We are fighting for recognition as free humans in this society." — Malcolm X

H e was born Malcolm Little; as a young man he was called Detroit Red; but the world remembers him as Malcolm X. Born in Omaha, Nebraska, he was the seventh of eleven children. His father, Reverend Earl Little, was a Baptist minister and a strong believer in Marcus Garvey's ideas of black independence and self-respect. These ideas did not sit well with the local Ku Klux Klan. As a result, after Malcolm's birth, the family moved, first to Milwaukee, Wisconsin, and later to Lansing, Michigan.

Unfortunately, Reverend Little's ideas were no more popular in Lansing than they had been in Omaha, and in 1929 members of a local vigilante group set fire to the Little's home. Malcolm's father was not one to be bullied, however. He stayed and built another home. But when Malcolm was six, his father was murdered, apparently by the same men who had burned his house.

Things were never the same after that. Malcolm quit school after the eighth grade. He traveled first to Boston, Massachusetts, and then to Harlem, New York, where he became involved in crime. In 1946, at the age of twenty-one, he was charged with burglary and sent to prison for six and a half years.

While in prison, he became interested in the Nation of Islam, popularly known as the Black Muslims. This religious group, led by Elijah Muhammad, promoted black economic independence and sought to establish a separate black state either in the United States or in Africa.

Malcolm joined the Black Muslims. According to custom, he dropped his original last name and called himself Malcolm X. Serious about the new religion, he studied its teachings with interest. He also began educating himself by reading the encyclopedia and memorizing words from the dictionary.

When Malcolm X was released from prison in 1952, he became a Muslim minister and spent the next twelve years organizing mosques and spreading the Black Muslim message. He condemned the nonviolent attempts of other black leaders to achieve integration, saying, "You can't stick a knife in a man's back nine inches and then pull it out six inches and say you're making progress." Many people were attracted by Malcolm X's ideas and supported him when he condemned the seemingly slow progress of the civil rights movement.

But Malcolm X's success as a speaker and as an organizer caused jealousy and resentment. In December 1963, Elijah Muhammad suspended him. Three months later, Malcolm X quit the Nation of Islam and organized his own group called the Organization of Afro-American Unity (OAAU).

In the summer of 1964, he traveled to the Middle East and to Africa to see how the Muslim religion was practiced there. Impressed, he converted to orthodox Islam and returned to the United States, denouncing Elijah Muhammad as a religious fake and a racist.

The Black Muslim newspaper, *Muhammad Speaks*, responded by calling Malcolm X a liar and saying he was "worthy of death." It was not a threat to be taken lightly. On February 15, 1965, Malcolm X's home was firebombed—just as his father's home had been thirty-six years before. One week later, on February 21, he was shot to death at a rally in the Audubon Ballroom in New York. Three Black Muslims were convicted of the murder, although the Nation of Islam officially denied having anything to do with his killing.

Malcolm X's death came as a great shock. To thousands of black people around the world, he personified revolution. He was able to appeal to ordinary people and to articulate the anger and frustration they felt. Above all, he symbolized unyielding defiance and resistance in the face of prejudice, discrimination, and repression.

The 1963 March on Washington

They came by car, and they came by plane—in 2,000 chartered buses and thirty special trains, on foot, on bicycles, and in wheelchairs. It was August 28, 1963, and 250,000 people had gathered in Washington, D.C., to protest that black people still were not free in America.

The idea for the march had come from Bayard Rustin, close friend and adviser to Asa Philip Randolph. Randolph felt that the sit-ins and protests being held throughout the South needed the backing of a massive, national demonstration—one that would show a unified demand for civil and economic rights. Rustin suggested a march involving all the civil rights organizations to bring attention to the need for jobs, a higher minimum wage, a guaranteed income, and full rights for everyone.

Earlier, in June, President John F. Kennedy had announced on nationwide television that he would submit a civil rights bill to Congress that would force owners of restaurants, hotels, theaters, and stores to serve any orderly person without regard to race. He opposed the Washington march, fearing it would create a backlash in Congress that would make his legislation harder to pass. But leaders of the March on Washington decided to forge ahead.

By 9:00 A.M., on the day of the march, 40,000 people were gathered at the base of the Washington Monument. An hour and a half later, more than 90,000 people covered the grounds. Speakers began to address the crowd. Floyd McKissick delivered a speech for James Farmer of CORE, who was in a Louisiana jail because of his civil rights activities. John Lewis of SNCC spoke angrily of "[splintering] the segregated South into a thousand pieces." Roy Wilkins of NAACP demanded passage of the civil rights bill. But it was the words of Dr. Martin Luther King, Jr., in his famous "I Have a Dream" speech, that echoed and reechoed across the country.*

*See pages 232-234 for Martin Luther King, Jr.'s speech "I Have a Dream."

Thousands who stood in the sweltering heat and listened to the words of freedom, responded with hope, faith, and determination. The future would be rocked by riots, war, and assassinations, but on this day, August 28, 1963, 100 years and 274 days after the signing of the Emancipation Proclamation, thousands of American citizens were standing together, reminding the nation and the world of what freedom really meant.

Marchers at the Lincoln Memorial, Washington, D.C., August 1963

Roy Wilkins

Civil Rights Leader
1901-1981

In 1932 Roy Wilkins was asked by the NAACP to investigate reports of racial discrimination against blacks working on a federally financed flood control project in Mississippi. Wilkins agreed, and, along with another NAACP worker, made his way south, not knowing what he would find.

Arriving in Mississippi, the two men dressed in old clothes and got jobs as laborers on the project. Working undercover, they quietly gathered the information they needed. They had the look; they had the walk; they had the talk. Only one thing was wrong, and it could have gotten them both killed. Roy Wilkins's hands were long and graceful and smooth—not the hands of a laborer. A white storekeeper noticed this and grew suspicious. But by that time, Wilkins and his companion had enough information to convince Congress to take action, and they quickly left.

Roy Wilkins was born in St. Louis, Missouri, on August 30, 1901. His mother died of tuberculosis when he was three years old. Together with his brother and sister, he was sent to live with an aunt and uncle in St. Paul, Minnesota. After graduating from high school, where he was editor of the school paper, Wilkins enrolled at the University of Minnesota. To help pay his tuition, he worked as a redcap, a waiter, and a clean-up man in the stockyards. He also edited the university newspaper and a black paper called the St. Paul *Appeal.* In his spare time, he served as secretary for the local branch of the NAACP.

After college, Wilkins went to work for the Kansas City (Missouri) *Call*, the city's leading black newspaper. For the first time, he found himself living in an area where there was widespread segregation. He responded by working harder for the NAACP and by leading a successful campaign against the reelection of a prosegregationist senator.

This work brought Roy Wilkins to the attention of NAACP leaders, and, in 1931, he was offered the job of assistant executive secretary. He was to remain an NAACP leader for forty-six years, becoming executive secretary in 1955.

During those years, the NAACP took legal action to overturn school segregation and to support civil rights legislation. Roy Wilkins played a major role in these activities, getting support for the 1964 Civil Rights Act, the 1965 Voting Rights Act, and the 1968 Fair Housing Act. He was a key organizer and supporter of the famous 1963 March on Washington. Under his leadership, the NAACP grew to include approximately 500,000 members with 1,700 chapters across the country. When thousands of protesters were arrested during the sit-ins, marches, and demonstrations of the 1950s and 1960s, the NAACP took the lead in providing bail money and legal and organizational support. Roy Wilkins was one of those arrested.

In defending the willingness of the protesters to engage in civil disobedience, he said, "We condemn the propaganda that Negro citizens must 'earn' their rights through good behavior. Good behavior ... wins the respect of our fellow citizens which we value and seek, but no American is required to 'earn' his rights as a citizen. His human rights come from God, and his citizenship rights come from the Constitution." These were rights Roy Wilkins spent his lifetime trying to protect.

Martin Luther King, Jr.

Author, Civil Rights Activist
1929-1968

"I have a dream that my four little children will one day live in a nation where they will not be judged by the color of their skin, but by the content of their character."
— Martin L. King, Jr.

In 1954 Martin Luther King, Jr., became pastor of the Dexter Avenue Baptist Church in Montgomery, Alabama. A year later, Rosa Parks was arrested there for refusing to give up her seat on a bus to a white man. Her arrest marked the beginning of Dr. King's lifelong struggle in the civil rights movement—a commitment that would bring him love, admiration, anger, and hate. It would demand his courage, his faith, his freedom, and, eventually, his life.

Martin Luther King, Jr., was born in Atlanta, Georgia, on January 15, 1929 and raised in a quiet, black middle-class neighborhood. His father, the pastor of Ebenezer Baptist Church in Atlanta, and his mother, a schoolteacher, were highly respected professionals in the black community.

Quick to learn, Martin entered Morehouse College when he was only fifteen years old. After graduation, he became an ordained minister and enrolled at Crozer Theological Seminary in Chester, Pennsylvania, for a masters degree. There he studied the teachings of Mahatma Gandhi, the leader who struggled to gain India's independence from England. King became convinced that nonviolent action was the way to bring about change.

After graduating from Crozer, King enrolled in the doctoral

program in philosophy at Boston University. While there, he met and married Coretta Scott. In 1954 they returned to Montgomery, where a position as pastor of Dexter Avenue Baptist Church was waiting for him.

On December 1, 1955, Rosa Parks was arrested for violating the city bus ordinance that required blacks to give up their seats to whites. Immediately, black ministers and civic leaders in Montgomery called a meeting at the Dexter Avenue Baptist Church. They agreed that a one-day bus boycott would take place on Monday, December 5. That Sunday, King and the others announced the boycott to their congregations and urged them to support it. Approximately 17,000 black people usually rode the buses each day. How many would support the boycott? As it turned out, almost all of them would.

To continue the boycott, black leaders set up the Montgomery Improvement Association with Dr. King as its leader. Angry racists responded by threatening black leaders. Threats turned into action when Dr. King's house was bombed in January.

The Montgomery Bus Boycott lasted 381 days and cost the bus company more than $750,000. Hundreds of black boycotters lost their jobs and many were thrown in jail. But they won. On November 13, 1957, the U.S. Supreme Court declared Alabama's laws requiring segregation on buses unconstitutional.

In order to keep the movement going, King met with southern black ministers in February 1957 and formed the Southern Christian Leadership Conference (SCLC). He was named its president. Guided by nonviolent philosophy and Christian beliefs, the SCLC was to become one of the dominant civil rights organizations in the South.

Drawing on the recognition he had gained as leader of the boycott, King began traveling around the country encouraging support of civil rights. In 1958 he wrote his first book, *Stride Toward Freedom*. Two weeks after it was published, he was stabbed by a mentally ill black woman. When he recovered, he and Coretta visited India. Shortly after their return, the King family moved to Atlanta, where Martin joined his father as copastor of the Ebenezer Baptist Church.

In February 1960, the student sit-in movement got under way in Greensboro, North Carolina. Student leaders set up SNCC to guide the protests, and the SCLC, under King's leadership, offered its support. King also gave his support to the CORE when it began its Freedom Rides to integrate interstate buses in 1961.

Meanwhile, demonstrators in Albany, Georgia, were supporting Freedom Riders and voter registration. In spite of the fact that hundreds had been arrested, the situation received little national attention. So Dr. King was asked to help. But after 2,000 Albany blacks rioted, it seemed as though Dr. King's nonviolent policy was finished. Frustrated by the rivalry of local black groups, King returned to Atlanta, determined to learn from the defeat.

In April 1963, King launched a campaign to stop segregation in Birmingham, Alabama, one of the South's most violent and segregated cities. He demanded desegregation of lunch counters, restrooms, and drinking fountains and the hiring of blacks by local businesses and the city government. After three days of demonstrations, police, using dogs, moved against the protesters. King was arrested, jailed, and placed in solitary confinement. Eight white clergymen signed a statement denouncing the protests and urging Birmingham's black ministers to show restraint.

King was dismayed. As a man of God he had hoped for the support of the white clergy even though their churches were still segregated. From his jail cell he wrote a 9,000-word appeal to his fellow ministers. This *Letter From Birmingham City Jail* became one of the most famous statements of the civil rights movement. * Thousands of copies were printed and read by people across the country. Shortly afterward, King was released and many of the charges against him were dropped. But Birmingham still hadn't changed its ways. Something dramatic was needed to capture the attention of the nation.

*See pages 227-231 for Martin Luther King, Jr.'s *Letter From Birmingham City Jail*.

On Thursday, May 2, a children's demonstration was scheduled. Hundreds of youngsters, ages six through sixteen, took part. Before the march was over, police had hauled 959 children off to jail. During the second day of the march, police hosed the children down with water. Many were knocked to the ground while police dogs attacked them. Americans who witnessed the attacks were furious.

President Kennedy immediately sent two officials from the Justice Department to negotiate a settlement. King had four demands: that all downtown stores be immediately desegregated; that blacks be hired as salespeople and clerks; that all demonstrators under arrest be released; and that a permanent biracial committee be set up. By the end of the week, city leaders gave in to all the demands.

Meanwhile, plans were being made for a march on Washington. Although its purpose was to build support for President Kennedy's civil rights bill, it became one of the turning points in the civil rights movement. Over 250,000 people (190,000 black and 60,000 white) came from all over the world. The triumphant gathering brought a climax but not an end to the civil rights movement. One month later, the Ku Klux Klan bombed the Sixteenth Street Baptist Church in Birmingham, killing four little girls.

The 1964 Civil Rights Act ended segregation in public places. But the bill did not deal with the problem of voting rights. And nowhere was that problem worse than in Mississippi. To encourage black voter registration, civil rights groups set up the Mississippi Summer Project. Nineteen hundred students (mostly white) from around the country volunteered.

On the night of June 21, three young CORE workers, Michael Schwerner, James Chaney, and Andrew Goodman, were murdered by the Klan. Over the course of the summer, four more civil rights people were murdered; thirty-five were shot, eighty were beaten, and 1,000 were arrested. Sixty-five churches and other buildings were either bombed or burned.

On December 10, Dr. King was awarded the Nobel Peace Prize. He donated some of the prize money to the civil rights movement.

Meanwhile, the SCLC was asked to come to Selma, Alabama, to take over a voter registration drive SNCC had begun a year earlier. On January 18, 1965, King led the first demonstration to the county courthouse without any incidents. But as the marches continued, state troopers became brutal. On February 18, a twenty-five-year-old black man named Jimmy Lee Jackson was killed when he tried to stop a state trooper from beating his mother.

King immediately announced plans for another march and invited Catholic nuns and priests, Protestant ministers, and Jewish rabbis from across the country. Hundreds of religious people marched. One of them, a white minister named James Reeb, was attacked. He died two days later. The violence in Selma caused President Lyndon Johnson to seek passage of a bill to guarantee black voting rights. Passed by Congress, the 1965 Voting Rights Act was signed into law on August 6.

Although the struggle for full civil rights in the South was far from complete, the Civil Rights Act of 1964 and the Voting Rights Act of 1965 provided a legal framework through which local black groups could work. Martin Luther King had provided the confidence and encouragement they needed to succeed. Now, it was time to take the movement North.

Deciding to concentrate on housing needs first, Dr. King moved into a rundown apartment in Chicago, Illinois. He then announced his plans to lead a rent strike if slum landlords did not upgrade their properties. He also set up Operation Breadbasket to promote black job opportunities. But the drive to eliminate slums in Chicago resulted in promises and not much else. Operation Breadbasket was more successful. Faced with boycotts, a number of businesses either went broke or agreed to hire blacks.

By 1965 national interest in civil rights had begun to fade as more people shifted their attention to the Vietnam War. President Johnson, who had once supported King, turned against him after King spoke out against the war. And many blacks, impatient with the slow progress of the nonviolent movement, were turning to violence.

But not everyone had lost faith in Dr. King. The sanitation workers in Memphis, Tennessee, asked for his help. Poor and mostly black, they had gone on strike in an effort to get the city to meet their demands. So far, they had been unsuccessful. They hoped that Dr. King's presence would make a difference.

Over the next few weeks, Dr. King worked to organize a series of nonviolent demonstrations to support the sanitation workers' demands.

On the evening of April 4, 1968, he walked out on the balcony of his motel room and was shot dead by James Earl Ray.

As news of his death flashed across TV screens and newspapers, riots broke out in American cities. Over 100,000 people stood outside the Ebenezer Baptist Church in Atlanta, where his funeral was being held. Thousands of speeches were made in tribute to him. But it is King's own words that echo the loudest. In a sermon he delivered a few months before his death, he said,

"There is, deep down within all of us, an instinct—a 'Drum Major' instinct, a desire to be out in front, a desire to lead the parade . . . . If any of you are around when I have to meet my day, I don't want a long funeral. And if you get somebody to deliver the eulogy, tell him not to talk too long . . . . I'd like somebody to mention on that day that Martin Luther King, Jr. . . . did try to feed the hungry . . . that I did try, in my life, to visit those who were in prison . . . that I tried to love and serve humanity. Yes, if you want to say that I was a Drum Major, say that I was a Drum Major for justice; say that I was a Drum Major for peace; that I was a Drum Major for righteousness."[8]

The Black Power Movement

The civil rights movement of the 1950s and 1960s was fueled by courage, determination, and the belief that at some point the promises of American democracy would be made good. But violence and the resistance of white people to the civil rights movement unleashed anger, frustration, and resentment in the black community.

The development of black political power and the gradual appearance of black elected officials were a direct result of the black voter registration campaigns of the civil rights movement. But it took years for these developments to become apparent. Much more rapid and visible progress was made in the desegregation of lunch counters, movie theatres, and other public places, but none of it came easy. As poverty and unemployment continued to gnaw at the black community, the Black Power Movement came into being.

Unlike the civil rights movement, which was guided by a coalition of organizations like CORE, SCLC, and the NAACP and directed toward definite goals, the Black Power Movement was a loosely drawn jumble of organizations and individuals united primarily by their rejection of white society and their appeal to black pride and black consciousness.

Most notable of the groups identified with the Black Power Movement was the Black Panther Party. Begun in 1966, it soon included 1,500 members in thirty-eight chapters. Based primarily in the large cities of the North and West, it helped to establish day-care centers and provide free breakfasts for poor people. Although its programs were not especially revolutionary, its rhetoric was. The bitter accusations of its leaders against whites in general and the police in particular resulted in hostility and bloodshed. A number of Panther members were involved in shoot-outs with the police. Two leaders were killed in Chicago when dozens of police shot up their apartment. The police argued self-defense, but later evidence threw considerable doubt on that claim.

The Black Muslims, or Nation of Islam (a religious group that preached black self-respect), also was identified with the Black Power Movement, thanks to Malcolm X, their most eloquent spokesman. His murder by fellow Muslims in 1965, however, cost the Nation of Islam much of its appeal.

Another group involved in the Black Power Movement was SNCC, the student organization that had been created to help guide the sit-ins. But in the late 1960s, some of its leaders, especially Stokely Carmichael, refused to work any longer with whites. These groups, though different, were similar in their antiwhite statements and their rejection of Martin Luther King's nonviolent philosophy. It was a rejection that King found painful.

Also upsetting to King were the riots that broke out in over 100 American cities in the late 1960s. The first took place in Watts in Los Angeles in 1965. Before it was over, thirty-four people were dead, 898 were injured, and 4,000 had been arrested. It set a pattern that was to be repeated in the long, hot summers ahead.

The riots shocked and frightened the nation, revealing the depth of black resentment that went beyond criminals and radicals. Many widely respected blacks showed the same resentment. Heavyweight champion Muhammad Ali made his feelings plain when he refused to fight in Vietnam, saying, "No Vietcong ever called me nigger." Olympic champions Timmy Smith and John Carlos raised their fists in the Black Power salute as they were about to receive their medals in 1968. Black people across the country began wearing African clothes and "natural" hairstyles to express their pride. The words "Black Power" and "Black Is Beautiful" were heard everywhere.

Although the Black Power Movement was attacked by those who felt that it destroyed white support for civil rights, it played a part in pressuring President Lyndon Johnson to declare a "War on Poverty." During his administration, dozens of programs were established to promote better health, education, jobs, and housing for poor people, many of them black. Although some of the programs failed, many were successful.

Guion Stewart Bluford, Jr.

Pilot, Astronaut
1942

"If you want to succeed, [you must] ...work hard, dedicate yourself and make the necessary sacrifices.... Once you set goals for yourself, you should doggedly pursue them until you achieve them." —Guion Bluford

Colonel Guion S. Bluford, Jr., sat strapped to his seat aboard the 100-ton space shuttle *Challenger* on August 30, 1983. A few minutes after 2:30 A.M., the *Challenger* blasted off, carrying the first black American astronaut into space.

Guion Bluford was born in Philadelphia in 1942. He joined the air force in 1964 and proceeded to fly 144 combat missions in Vietnam. He logged more than 3,000 hours of flying time and was awarded more than two dozen medals and awards. But Bluford wanted to do more than fly airplanes. He wanted to design them as well.

Soon after returning from Vietnam, he was accepted at the U.S. Air Force Institute of Technology, where he earned a masters degree in aerospace engineering. Then he began testing new airplanes and evaluating new aircraft systems.

In 1978 Bluford received his Ph.D. in aerospace engineering with a minor in laser physics. The same year he applied for admittance to the astronaut program with the National Aeronautics and Space Administration (NASA). Although 8,878 people had applied, there were only thirty-five openings. Guion Bluford was selected to fill one of them.

Training took place at the Johnson Space Flight Center in Houston,

Texas. For six months, Bluford attended classes in aerodynamics, medicine, astronomy, geology, and communications. He spent weeks learning to operate the space shuttle's remote manipulator and working with computers, power systems, and instruments that controlled the shuttle's ascents, descents, reentry, and orbital movements.

America's space program had gotten under way in 1957 when the Soviet Union launched Sputnik I, a 184-pound space satellite. The U. S. public was shocked at the Russian "first," and within a year, NASA was created. In 1961 the Soviet Union scored another first when Yuri Gagarin became the first man to orbit the earth. Twenty-three days later, the U. S. launched its first man in space—Commander Alan B. Shepard. By the time Guion Bluford entered the astronaut program, America had taken the lead in space exploration.

In August 1983, he joined the crew aboard the *Challenger*, the second U.S. space shuttle, and began a six-day flight in space, 180 miles above the earth. During the flight, Bluford launched a forty-five-million-dollar Insat 1B communications and weather satellite for India and participated in medical tests to discover why some astronauts experience motion sickness. Bluford and the *Challenger* crew landed on September 5 at Edwards Air Force Base in California.

On October 30, 1985, he was a crew member on another *Challenger* mission. This one involved 111 orbits of the earth during which seventy-six scientific experiments were performed.

At the completion of this mission, Lieutenant Colonel Bluford had logged 314 hours in space. His preparation for the space flight, however, had consisted of thousands of hours of dedicated work and study on earth.

Toni Morrison
Novelist, Editor
1931

Beloved
you are my sister
you are my daughter
You are my face; you are me[9]

"She paints pictures with words, and reading or hearing those words is like listening to music." These words of Leontyne Price refer to Toni Morrison, one of the best writers of the twentieth century.

Born in Lorain, Ohio, in 1931, Toni Morrison was christened Chloe Anthony Wofford. Her mother's family were sharecroppers from Greenville, Alabama, who moved north after losing their land. Her father's family came from Georgia.

Toni's early life was filled with tales of other worlds and other times. Some she heard from her grandmother, who conscientiously kept a record of her dreams in a small notebook. Others she heard from her parents, who were wonderful storytellers. Like roots of a tree, memories of these childhood songs, stories, and folklore were to nourish and support the creations of her own imagination.

When Toni started school, she was the only black child in her first grade class and the only one who could read. Her love of reading continued into adolescence as she immersed herself in the great American and Russian novels.

Encouraged by her family to excel, Toni finished high school and went on to receive a B.A. degree from Howard University in 1953.

Two years later, she received an M.A. from Cornell University and returned to Howard to teach and to write. While there, she met Harold Morrison, an architecture student from Jamaica, and married him.

Soon after her second son was born, Toni Morrison began working as a textbook editor in Syracuse, New York. Later, she became senior editor at Random House, a publishing company in New York. Her position allowed her to help and encourage many young black writers and to arrange for the publication of books on black history.

But it was her own writing that established her as an important person in American literature. Her first four novels—*The Bluest Eye*, *Sula*, *Song of Solomon* (which won the National Book Critics Circle Award), and *Tar Baby*—reflect both the pain and the beauty of the black American experience. Her fifth novel, *Beloved*, won the Pulitzer Prize for Literature in 1988. Based on the true story of a slave named Margaret Garner, who killed her own daughter rather than see her live as a slave, *Beloved* is an intensely felt ghost story laced with sorrow, poetry, and pain.

Toni Morrison's genius as a writer lies in her ability to draw her readers into the worlds she creates. The emotions she calls forth tie us to her characters, forcing us to feel their loneliness and their love.

> I have found you again; you have come back to me
> You are my Beloved
> You are mine
> You are mine
> You are mine[10]

Jesse Jackson

Minister, Civil Rights Leader
1941

"America is like a quilt—many patches, many pieces, many colors, many sizes, all woven and held together by a common thread.... all of us count and fit somewhere ...."—Jesse Jackson

"I am somebody!" Young black people throughout the country shout that slogan, repeating the words of Jesse Jackson who is a special somebody not only in their eyes but also in the eyes of the world.

Born in Greenville, South Carolina, Jesse Jackson graduated from Sterling High School and received a football scholarship to the University of Illinois. Not long after enrolling there, he transferred to North Carolina Agricultural and Technical College at Greensboro and became active in the sit-in-movement.

After graduating with a B.A., Jackson entered the Chicago Theological Seminary and continued his involvement in the civil rights movement. In 1965 he met Dr. Martin Luther King, Jr., at the famous Selma March and became a member of the SCLC staff. Then, returning to Chicago, he began to prepare for King's "Campaign to End Slums."

The same year, Jackson was made head of the Chicago branch of Operation Breadbasket, an organization established by Martin Luther King in 1962 and modeled after one previously developed by Reverend Leon Sullivan of Philadelphia. One of its purposes was to expand job opportunities for blacks.

Operation Breadbasket was very successful under Jesse Jackson's direction. Businesses that discriminated against blacks were boycotted—a tactic that proved very effective. Within a short time, many companies agreed to hire black employees, contract with black-owned service companies, and utilize black-owned banks.

Resigning from SCLC and Operation Breadbasket in 1971, Jackson founded Operation PUSH (People United to Serve Humanity). It aimed at improving the economic status of blacks. Again threatening to boycott businesses, Jackson persuaded many national companies, such as Burger King, to set up black distributorships and to spend millions of dollars advertising in black newspapers and magazines.

Over the next few years, several branches of PUSH were established. In 1976 Jackson began PUSH for Excellence, a program designed to help black students get a better education.

Realizing that black economic growth depended on having black political power, Jackson began touring the country to encourage voter registration. Everywhere, he preached the same message: use the power of the ballot box to elect officials who will be sympathetic to the needs of the poor, blacks in particular. Support black political power.

Eventually, Jackson, like Dr. King, became interested in international affairs. In 1979, with the hope of establishing dialogue among the Jews, Arabs, Palestinians, and other hostile groups in the Middle East, Jackson traveled to Israel, Lebanon, Egypt, and Syria. He met with Egyptian President Anwar Sadat, Syrian President Hafez al-Assad, and Palestinian leader Yassar Arafat. In terms of bringing about an Arab-Israeli peace, he accomplished little. But his personal contact with Syrian leader Assad proved to be helpful.

In 1984 Jackson used his friendship with Assad to obtain the release of U.S. Navy pilot Robert Goodman, who was taken prisoner after his plane was shot down during U.S. military operations in Lebanon. The same year, Jackson visited Cuba and obtained the release of twenty-two Americans and twenty-six Cubans who were being held prisoner.

The year 1984 was significant for Jesse Jackson for another reason, also. It was the year he first tried to capture the Democratic nomination for president of the United States. A black presidential campaign was needed, he said, to prove that the civil rights movement had not died with Dr. King. And it was time to demonstrate to politicians, both Democrats and Republicans, that the concerns of black people could not be ignored.

The idea of a black candidate was not new. Black congresswoman Shirley Chisholm had sought the Democratic nomination twelve years earlier. But Jesse Jackson was the first to mount a major challenge.

Although he was the clear favorite among blacks, receiving as much as 79 percent to 87 percent of the black vote, Jackson needed white votes as well if he were to win the nomination. So he put together what he called the "Rainbow Coalition" and began addressing the concerns of women, Hispanics, the poor, the handicapped, the young, and, in general, everyone who felt they were being ignored by the other candidates.

By the time of the Democratic convention in San Francisco, Jackson had the support of more than 450 delegates. It wasn't enough to win, but it was impressive.

In 1988 Jackson again sought the Democratic nomination. This time, he ran even stronger than before. Previously, many political leaders had scoffed at the idea of a successful black presidential candidate. The country was not ready, they said. But Jesse Jackson showed them up. "Excellence is doing your best against the odds," he said. "As I run for president . . . I run against the odds, and yet I defy the odds." The 1988 campaign proved Jackson's point. He enlarged his base of black support while gathering thousands of white votes. Though he didn't win, he came close. In doing so, Jesse Jackson forced the country to take seriously the idea of a black president and insured the continuance of black political power.

The Emancipation Proclamation
(1863)

BY THE PRESIDENT OF THE UNITED STATES OF AMERICA:

A Proclamation.

Whereas on the 22d day of September, A.D. 1862, a proclamation was issued by the President of the United States, containing, among other things, the following, to wit:

"That on the 1st day of January A.D. 1863, all persons held as slaves within any State or designated part of a State the people whereof shall then be in rebellion against the United States shall be then, thenceforward, and forever free; and the executive government of the United States, including the military and naval authority thereof, will recognize and maintain the freedom of such persons and will do no act or acts to repress such persons, or any of them, in any efforts they may make for their actual freedom.

"That the executive will on the 1st day of January aforesaid, by proclamation, designate the States and parts of States, if any, in which the people thereof, respectively, shall then be in rebellion against the United States; and the fact that any State or the people thereof shall on that day be in good faith represented in the Congress of the United States by members chosen thereto at elections wherein a majority of the qualified voters of such States shall have participated shall, in the absence of strong countervailing testimony, be deemed conclusive evidence that such State and the people thereof are not then in rebellion against the United States."

Now, therefore, I, Abraham Lincoln, President of the United States, by virtue of the power in me vested as Commander-in-Chief of the Army and Navy of the United States in time of actual armed rebellion against the authority and government of the United States, and as a fit and neccessary war measure for suppressing said rebellion, do, on this 1st day of January, A.D. 1863, and in accordance with my purpose so to do, publicly proclaimed for the full period of one hundred days from the first day above mentioned, order and designate as the States and parts of States wherein the people thereof, respectively, are this day in rebellion against the United States the following, to wit:

Arkansas, Texas, Louisiana (except the parishes of St. Bernard, Plaquemines, Jefferson, St. John, St. Charles, St. James, Ascension, Assumption, Terrebonne, Lafourche, St. Mary, St. Martin, and Orleans, including the city of New Orleans), Mississippi, Alabama, Florida, Georgia, South Carolina, North Carolina, and Virginia (except the forty-eight counties designated as West Virginia, and also the counties of Berkeley, Accomac, Northampton, Elizabeth City, York, Princess Anne, and Norfolk, including the cities of Norfolk and Portsmouth), and which excepted parts are the present left precisely as if this proclamation were not issued.

And by virtue of the power and for the purpose aforesaid, I do order and declare that all persons held as slaves within said designated States and parts of States are, and henceforward shall be, free; and that the Executive Government of the United States, including the military and naval authorities thereof, will recognize and maintain the freedom of said persons.

And I hereby enjoin upon the people so declared to be free to abstain from all violence, unless in necessary self-defense; and I recommend to them that, in all cases when allowed, they labor faithfully for reasonable wages.

And I further declare and make known that such persons of suitable condition will be received into the armed service of the United States to garrison forts, positions, stations, and other places, and to man vessels of all sorts in said service.

And upon this act, sincerely believed to be an act of justice, warranted by the Constitution upon military necessity, I invoke the considerate judgment of mankind and the gracious favor of Almighty God.[11]

Reconstruction Amendments to the U.S. Constitution

Amendment XIII

Section 1 Neither slavery nor involuntary servitude, except as a punishment for crime whereof the party shall have been duly convicted, shall exist within the United States, or any place subject to their jurisdiction.

Section 2 Congress shall have power to enforce this article by appropriate legislation. [Adopted in 1865.]

Amendment XIV

Section 1 All persons born or naturalized in the United States, and subject to the jurisdiction thereof, are citizens of the United States and of the State wherein they reside. No State shall make or enforce any law which shall abridge the privileges or immunities of citizens of the United States; nor shall any State deprive any person of life, liberty, or property, without due process of law; nor deny to any person within its jurisdiction the equal protection of the laws.

Section 2 Representatives shall be apportioned among the several States according to their respective numbers, counting the whole number of persons in each State excluding Indians not taxed. But when the right to vote at any election for the choice of electors for President and Vice President of the United States, Representatives in Congress, the Executive and Judicial officers of a State, or the members of the Legislature thereof, is denied to any of the male inhabitants of such State, being twenty-one years of age, and citizens of the United States, or in any way abridged, except for participation in rebellion, or other crime, the basis of representation therein shall be reduced in the proportion which the number of such male citizens shall bear to the whole number of male citizens twenty-one years of age in such State.

Section 3 No person shall be a Senator or Representative in Congress, or elector of President and Vice President, or hold any office, civil or military, under the United States, or under any State, who, having previously taken an oath, as a member of Congress, or as an officer of the United States, or as a member of any State legislature, or as an executive or judicial officer of any State, to support the Constitution of the United States, shall have engaged in insurrection or rebellion against the same, or given aid or comfort to the enemies thereof. But Congress may by a vote of two-thirds of each House, remove such disability.

Section 4 The validity of the public debt of the United States, authorized by law, including debts incurred for payment of pensions and bounties for services in suppressing insurrection or rebellion, shall not be questioned. But neither the United States nor any State shall assume or pay any debt or obligation incurred in aid or insurrection or rebellion against the United States, or any claim for the loss or emancipation of any slave; but all such debts, obligations and claims shall be held illegal and void.

Section 5 The Congress shall have power to enforce, by appropriate legislation, the provision of this article. [Adopted in 1868.]

Amendment XV

Section 1 The right of citizens of the United States to vote shall not be denied or abridged by the United States or by any State on account of race, color, or previous condition of servitude.

Section 2 The Congress shall have power to enforce this article by appropriate legislation. [Adopted in 1870.][12]

Elizabeth Eckford's Account of Day One at Central High School

"You remember the day before we were to go in, we met Superintendent Blossom at the school board office. He told us what the mob might say and do but he never told us we wouldn't have any protection. He told our parents not to come because he wouldn't be able to protect the children if they did.

"That night I was so excited I couldn't sleep. The next morning I was about the first one up. While I was pressing my black and white dress—I had made it to wear on the first day of school—my little brother turned on the TV set. They started telling about a large crowd gathered at the school. . . .

"Before I left home Mother called us into the living-room. She said we should have a word of prayer. Then I caught the bus and got off a block from the school. I saw a large crowd of people standing across the street from the soldiers guarding Central. As I walked on, the crowd suddenly got very quiet. Superintendent Blossom had told us to enter by the front door. I looked at all the people and thought, 'Maybe I will be safer if I walk down the block to the front entrance behind the guards.'

"At the corner I tried to pass through the long line of guards around the school so as to enter the grounds behind them. One of the guards pointed across the street. So I pointed in the same direction and asked whether he meant for me to cross the street and walk down. He nodded 'yes.' So, I walked across the street conscious of the crowd that stood there, but they moved away from me.

"For a moment all I could hear was the shuffling of their feet. Then someone shouted, 'Here she comes, get ready!' I moved away from the crowd on the sidewalk and into the street. If the mob came at me I could then cross back over so the guards could protect me.

"The crowd moved in closer and then began to follow me, calling me names, I still wasn't afraid. Just a little bit nervous. Then my knees started to shake all of a sudden and I wondered whether I could make it to the center entrance a block away. It was the longest block I ever walked in my whole life.

"Even so, I still wasn't too scared because all the time I kept thinking that the guards would protect me.

"When I got right in front of the school, I went up to a guard again. But this time he just looked straight ahead and didn't move to let me pass him. I didn't know what to do. Then I looked and saw that the path leading to the front entrance was a little further ahead. So I walked until I was right in front of the path to the front door.

"I stood looking at the school—it looked so big! Just then the guards let some white students go through.

"The crowd was quiet. I guess they were waiting to see what was going to happen. When I was able to steady my knees, I walked up to the guard who had let the white students in. He too didn't move. When I tried to squeeze past him, he raised his bayonet and then the other guards closed in and they raised their bayonets.

Elizabeth Eckford outside Central High School in Little Rock, Arkansas

"They glared at me with a mean look and I was very frightened and didn't know what to do. I turned around and the crowd came toward me.

"They moved closer and closer. Somebody started yelling, 'Lynch her! Lynch her!'

"I tried to see a friendly face somewhere in the mob—someone who maybe would help. I looked into the face of an old woman and it seemed a kind face, but when I looked at her again, she spat on me.

"They came closer, shouting, 'No nigger bitch is going to get in our school. Get out of here!'

"I turned back to the guards but their faces told me I wouldn't get help from them. Then I looked down the block and saw a bench at the bus stop. I thought, 'If I can only get there I will be safe.' I don't know why the bench seemed a safe place to me, but I started walking toward it. I tried to close my mind to what they were shouting, and kept saying to myself, 'If I can only make it to the bench I will be safe.'

"When I finally got there, I don't think I could have gone another step. I sat down and the mob crowded up and began shouting all over again. Someone hollered, 'Drag her over to this tree! Let's take care of the nigger.' Just then a white man sat down beside me, put his arm around me and patted my shoulder. He raised my chin and said, 'Don't let them see you cry.'

"Then, a white lady—she was very nice—she came over to me on the bench. She spoke to me but I don't remember now what she said. She put me on the bus and sat next to me. She asked me my name and tried to talk to me but I don't think I answered. I can't remember much about the bus ride, but the next thing I remember I was standing in front of the School for the Blind, where Mother works.

"I thought, 'Maybe she isn't here. But she has to be here!' So I ran upstairs, and I think some teachers tried to talk to me, but I kept running until I reached Mother's classroom.

"Mother was standing at the window with her head bowed, but she must have sensed I was there because she turned around. She looked as if she had been crying, and I wanted to tell her I was all right. But I couldn't speak. She put her arms around me and I cried."[13]

Letter from Birmingham City Jail
(April 16, 1963)

My dear fellow clergymen:

While confined here in the Birmingham city jail, I came across your recent statement calling my present activities "unwise and untimely." Seldom do I pause to answer criticism of my work and ideas. . . . But since I feel that you are men of genuine good will and that your criticisms are sincerely set forth, I want to try to answer your statement in what I hope will be patient and reasonable terms. . . .

I think I should indicate why I am here in Birmingham, since you have been influenced by the view which argues against "outsiders coming in.". . . I am here because I have organizational ties here. . . . But more basically, I am in Birmingham because injustice is here. . . .

Moreover, I am cognizant of the interrelatedness of all communities and states. I cannot sit idly by in Atlanta and not be concerned about what happens in Birmingham. Injustice anywhere is a threat to justice everywhere. We are caught in an inescapable network of mutuality, tied in a single garment of destiny.

Whatever affects one directly, affects all indirectly. Never again can we afford to live with the narrow, provincial "outside agitator" idea. Anyone who lives inside the United States can never be considered an outsider anywhere within its bounds.

You deplore the demonstrations taking place in Birmingham. But your statement, I am sorry to say, fails to express a similar concern for the conditions that brought about the demonstrations.

I am sure that none of you would want to rest content with the superficial kind of social analysis that deals merely with effects and does not grapple with underlying causes. It is unfortunate that demonstrations are taking place in Birmingham, but it is even more unfortunate that the city's white power structure left the Negro community with no alternative. . . .

There can be no gainsaying the fact that racial injustice engulfs this community. Birmingham is probably the most thoroughly segregated city in the United States. Its ugly record of brutality is widely known. Negroes have experienced grossly unjust treatment in the courts. There have been more unsolved bombings of Negro homes and churches in Birmingham than in any other city in the nation. These are the hard, brutal facts of the case. . . .

We have waited for more than 340 years for our constitutional and God-given rights. The nations of Asia and Africa are moving with jet-like speed toward gaining political independence, but we still creep at horse-and-buggy pace toward gaining a cup of coffee at a lunch counter. Perhaps it is easy for those who have never felt the stinging darts of segregation to say, "Wait."

But when you have seen vicious mobs lynch your mothers and fathers at will and drown your sisters and brothers at whim;

when you have seen hate-filled policemen curse, kick and even kill your black brothers and sisters;

when you see the vast majority of your twenty million Negro brothers smothering in an airtight cage of poverty in the midst of an affluent society:

when you suddenly find your tongue twisted and your speech stammering as you seek to explain to your six-year-old daughter why she can't go to the public amusement park that has just been advertised on television, and see tears welling up in her eyes when she is told that Funtown is closed to colored children, and see ominous clouds of inferiority beginning to form in her little mental sky, and see her beginning to distort her personality by developing an unconscious bitterness toward white people;

when you have to concoct an answer for a five-year-old son who is asking, "Daddy, why do white people treat colored people so mean?";

when you take a cross-country drive and find it necessary to sleep night after night in the uncomfortable corners of your automobile because no motel will accept you;

when you are humiliated day in and day out by nagging signs reading "white" and "colored";

when your first name becomes "nigger," your middle name becomes "boy" (however old you are) and your last becomes "John," and your wife and mother are never given the respected title "Mrs.";

when you are harried by day and haunted by night by the fact that you are a Negro, living constantly at tiptoe stance, never quite knowing what to expect next, and are plagued with inner fears and outer resentments;

when you are forever fighting a degenerating sense of "nobodiness"—then you will understand why we find it difficult to wait.

There comes a time when the cup of endurance runs over, and men are no longer willing to be plunged into the abyss of despair. I hope, sirs, you can understand our legitimate and unavoidable impatience. . . .

Throughout Alabama all sorts of devious methods are used to prevent Negroes from becoming registered voters, and there are some counties in which, even though Negroes constitute a majority of the population, not a single Negro is registered. Can any law enacted under such circumstances be considered democratically structured?

Sometimes a law is just on its face and unjust in it application. For instance, I have been arrested on a charge of parading without a permit. Now, there is nothing wrong in having an ordinance which requires a permit for a parade. But such an ordinance becomes unjust when it is used to maintain segregation and to deny citizens the First-Amendment privilege of peaceful assembly and protest.

I hope you are able to see the distinction I am trying to point out. In no sense do I advocate evading or defying the law, as would the rabid segregationist. That would lead to anarchy.

One who breaks an unjust law must do so openly, lovingly and with a willingness to accept the penalty. I submit that an individual who breaks a law that conscience tells him is unjust, and who willingly accepts the penalty of imprisonment in order to arouse the conscience of the community over its injustice, is in reality expressing the highest respect for law. . . .

You speak of our activity in Birmingham as extreme. At first I was rather disappointed that fellow clergymen would see my nonviolent efforts as those of an extremist. I began thinking about the fact that I stand in the middle of two opposing forces in the Negro community.

One is a force of complacency, made up in part of Negroes who, as a result of long years of oppression, are so drained of self-respect and a sense of "somebodiness" that they have adjusted to segregation; and in part of a few middle-class Negroes who, because of a degree of academic and economic security and because in some ways they profit by segregation, have become insensitive to the problems of the masses.

The other force is one of bitterness and hatred, and it comes perilously close to advocating violence. It is expressed in the various black nationalist groups that are springing up across the nation, the largest and best-known being Elijah Muhammad's Muslim movement. Nourished by the Negro's frustration over the continued existence of racial discrimination, this movement is made up of people who have lost faith in America, who have absolutely repudiated Christianity, and who have concluded that the white man is an incorrigible "devil."

I have tried to stand between these two forces, saying that we need emulate neither the "donothingism" of the complacent nor the hatred and despair of the black nationalist. For there is the more excellent way of love and nonviolent protest. I am grateful to God that, through the influence of the Negro church, the way of nonviolence became an integral part of our struggle.

If this philosophy had not emerged, by now many streets of the South would, I am convinced, be flowing with blood. And I am further convinced that if our white brothers dismiss as "rabble-rouser" and "outside agitators" those of us who employ nonviolent direct action, and if they refuse to support our nonviolent efforts, millions of Negroes will, out of frustration and despair, seek solace and security in black-nationalist ideologies—a development that would inevitably lead to a frightening racial nightmare. . . .

If one recognizes this vital urge that has engulfed the Negro community, one should readily understand why public demonstrations are taking place. The Negro has many pent-up resentments and latent frustrations, and he must release them. So let him march; let him make prayer pilgrimages to the city hall; let him go on freedom rides—and try to understand why he must do so. . . .

I wish you had commended the Negro sit-inners and demonstrators of Birmingham for their sublime courage, their willingness to suffer, and their amazing discipline in the midst of great provocation. One day the South will recognize its real heroes. They will be the James Merediths, with the noble sense of purpose that enables them to face jeering and hostile mobs, and with the agonizing loneliness that characterizes the life of the pioneer. They will be old, oppressed, battered Negro women, symbolized in a seventy-two-year-old woman in Montgomery, Alabama, who rose up with a sense of dignity and with her people decided not to ride segregated buses, and who responded with ungrammatical profundity to one who inquired about her weariness: "My feets is tired, but my soul is at rest."

They will be the young high school and college students, the young ministers of the gospel and a host of their elders, courageously and nonviolently sitting in at lunch counters and willingly going to jail for conscience' sake. One day the South will know that when these disinherited children of God sat down at lunch counters, they were in reality standing up for what is best in the American dream and for the most sacred values in our Judaeo-Christian heritage, thereby bringing our nation back to those great wells of democracy which were dug deep by the founding fathers in their formulation of the Constitution and the Declaration of Independence.

. . . .Let us all hope that the dark clouds of racial prejudice will soon pass away and the deep fog of misunderstanding will be lifted from our fear-drenched communities and in some not too distant tomorrow the radiant stars of love and brotherhood will shine over our great nation with all of their scintillating beauty.

Yours for the cause of Peace and Brotherhood,
Martin Luther King, Jr.[14]

"I Have a Dream" Speech

Five score years ago, a great American, in whose symbolic shadow we stand, signed the Emancipation Proclamation. This momentous decree came as a great beacon light of hope to millions of Negro slaves who had been seared in the flames of withering injustice. It came as a joyous daybreak to end the long night of captivity.

But one hundred years later, we must face the tragic fact that the Negro is still not free. One hundred years later, the life of the Negro is still sadly crippled by the manacles of segregation and the chains of discrimination. One hundred years later, the Negro lives on a lonely island of poverty in the midst of a vast ocean of material prosperity. One hundred years later, the Negro is still languished in the corners of American society and finds himself an exile in his own land. So we have come here today to dramatize an appalling condition.

In a sense we have come to our nation's Capitol to cash a check. When the architects of our republic wrote the magnificent words of the Constitution and the Declaration of Independence, they were signing a promissory note to which every American was to fall heir. This note was a promise that all men would be guaranteed the inalienable rights of life, liberty, and the pursuit of happiness.

It is obvious today that America has defaulted on this promissory note insofar as her citizens of color are concerned. Instead of honoring this sacred obligation, America has given the Negro people a bad check; a check which has come back marked "insufficient funds." But we refuse to believe that there are insufficient funds in the great vaults of opportunity of this nation. So we have come to cash this check—a check that will give us upon demand the riches of freedom and the security of justice. We have also come to this hallowed spot to remind America of the fierce urgency of *now*. This is no time to engage in the luxury of cooling off or to take the tranquilizing drug of gradualism. *Now* is the time to make real the promises of Democracy. *Now* is the time to rise from the dark and desolate valley of segregation to the sunlit path of racial justice. *Now* is the time to open the doors of opportunity to all of God's children. *Now* is the time to lift our nation from the quicksands of racial injustice to the solid rock of brotherhood.

It would be fatal for the nation to overlook the urgency of the moment and to underestimate the determination of the Negro. This sweltering summer of the Negro's legitimate discontent will not pass until there is an invigorating autumn of freedom and equality. 1963 is not an end, but a beginning. Those who hope that the Negro needed to blow off steam and will now be content will have a rude awakening if the Nation returns to business as usual. There will be neither rest nor tranquility in America until the Negro is granted his citizenship rights. The whirlwinds of revolt will continue to shake the foundations of our Nation until the bright day of justice emerges.

But there is something that I must say to my people who stand on the warm threshold which leads into the palace of justice. In the process of gaining our rightful place we must not be guilty of wrongful deeds. Let us not seek to satisfy our thirst for freedom by drinking from the cup of bitterness and hatred.

We must forever conduct our struggle on the high plane of dignity and discipline. We must not allow our creative protest to degenerate into physical violence. Again and again we must rise to the majestic heights of meeting physical force with soul force. The marvelous new militancy which has engulfed the Negro community must not lead us to a distrust of all white people, for many of our white brothers, as evidenced by their presence here today, have come to realize that their destiny is tied up with our destiny and their freedom is inextricably bound to our freedom. We cannot walk alone.

And as we walk, we must make the pledge that we shall march ahead. We cannot turn back. There are those who are asking the devotees of civil rights, "when will you be satisfied?" We can never be satisfied as long as the Negro is the victim of the unspeakable horrors of police brutality. We can never be satisfied as long as our bodies, heavy with the fatigue of travel, cannot gain lodging in the motels of the highways and the hotels of the cities. We cannot be satisfied as long as the Negro's basic mobility is from a smaller ghetto to a larger one. We can never be satisfied as long as a Negro in Mississippi cannot vote and a Negro in New York believes he has nothing for which to vote. No, no we are not satisfied, and we will not be satisfied until justice rolls down like waters and righteousness like a mighty stream. . . .

I say to you today, my friends, that in spite of the difficulties and frustrations of the moment I still have a dream. It is a dream deeply rooted in the American dream.

I have a dream that one day this nation will rise up and live out the true meaning of its creed: "We hold these truths to be self-evident; that all men are created equal."

I have a dream that one day on the red hills of Georgia the sons of former slaves and the sons of former slaveowners will be able to sit down together at the table of brotherhood.

I have a dream that one day even the state of Mississippi, a desert state sweltering with the heat of injustice and oppression, will be transformed into an oasis of freedom and justice.

I have a dream that my four little children will one day live in a nation where they will not be judged by the color of their skin but by the content of their character.

I have a dream that one day the state of Alabama, whose governor's lips are presently dripping with the words of interposition and nullification, will be transformed into a situation where little black boys and black girls will be able to join hands with little white boys and white girls and walk together as sisters and brothers. . . .

This will be the day when all of God's children will be able to sing with new meaning "My country 'tis of thee, sweet land of liberty, of thee I sing. Land where my fathers died, land of the pilgrim's pride, from every mountainside, let freedom ring. . . ."

When we let freedom ring, when we let it ring from every village and every hamlet, from every state and every city, we will be able to speed up that day when all of God's children, black men and white men, Jews and Gentiles, Protestants and Catholics, will be able to join hands and sing in the words of the old Negro spiritual, "Free at last! free at last! thank God almighty, we are free at last!"[15]

Footnotes

1. Sheldon, George, "Negro Slavery in Old Deerfield," *New England Magazine* (March 1893).

2. Ibid.

3. Billington, Ray Allen, ed., *The Journal of Charlotte L. Forten, A Free Negro in the Slave Era* (New York: Dryden Press, Inc., 1953).

4. Hughes, Langston, *The Panther and the Lash: Poems of Our Times* (New York: Alfred A. Knopf, 1974). Reprinted by permission of the publisher.

5. Cleveland *Call and Post* (April 15, 1937); "Olympic Games," *Time* (August 17, 1936), p.34; New York *Times* (January 27, 1950); Moro's interview with Owens.

6. Chicago *Defender* (September 26, 1942). Reprinted by permission of Publisher.

7. New York *Herald Tribune* (May 9, 1947).

8. Washington, James M., ed., *A Testament of Hope, The Essential Writings of Martin Luther King, Jr.* (San Francisco: Harper & Row, 1986), 259-267. Reprinted by permission of Joan Daves, © 1963 by Martin Luther King, Jr.

9. Morrison, Toni, *Beloved* (New York: Alfred A. Knopf, 1988), 216. Reprinted by permission of publisher.

10. Ibid

11. Commager, Henry Steele, ed., *Documents of American History to 1898*, Vol. 1 (Englewood Cliffs, New Jersey: Prentice-Hall, 1938), 420.

12. Ibid., 501.

13. Friedman, Leon, ed., *Civil Rights Reader: Basic Documents in the Civil Rights Movement* (New York: Walker & Company, 1967), 164-166.

14. King, Martin Luther, Jr., *Why We Can't Wait* (New York: Harper & Row, publishers, 1964), 52-59. Reprinted by permission of publisher.

15. Washington, James M., ed., op. cit. pp. 217-220.

16. Hughes, Langston, op. cit. p. 14.

Selected Bibliography

The author wishes to thank Dr. Walter Fisher Professor Emeritus of History and former library director, Morgan State University, for his bibliographic assistance.

Aptheker, Herbert. *American Negro Slave Revolts.* New York: International Publishers. 1969.

Bennett, Lerone. *Wade in the Water: Great Moments in Black History.* Chicago: Johnson Publishing Company, 1979.

Cornish, Dudley Taylor. *The Sable Arm, Negro Troops in the Union Army, 1861-1865.* New York: W.W. Norton & Company, 1966.

Davis, Burke. *Black Heroes of the American Revolution.* New York: Harcourt Brace Jovanovich, 1976.

Drotning, Phillip T. *Black Heroes in Our Nation's History.* New York: Dowles Book Company, 1969.

Franklin, John Hope and August Meier., eds. *Black Leaders of the Twentieth Century.* Urbana: University of Illinois Press, 1982.

Franklin, John Hope. *From Slavery to Freedom: A History of Negro Americans.* New York: Alfred A. Knopf, 1974.

Friedman, Leon., ed. *The Civil Rights Reader—Basic Documents of the Civil Rights Movement.* New York: Walker & Company, 1967.

Haber, Louis. *Black Pioneers of Science and Invention.* New York: Harcourt Brace Jovanovich, 1979.

Hansberry, Lorraine. *To Be Young, Gifted and Black, An Informal Autobiography of Lorraine Hansberry.* Adapted by Robert Nemiroff. New York: New American Library, 1969.

Harding, Vincent. *There Is a River, The Black Struggle for Freedom in America.* New York: Harcourt Brace Jovanovich, 1981.

Hayden, Robert C. *Eight Black American Inventors.* Reading, Massachusetts: Addison-Wesley Publishing Company, 1972.

Hughes, Langston. *Selected Poems of Langston Hughes.* New York: Alfred A. Knopf, 1959.

Hughes, Langston, Milton Meltzer & C. Erik Lincoln., eds. *A Pictorial History of Black Americans.* Fourth Edition. New York: Crown Publishers, 1983.

Katz, William Loren. *Black Indians,* New York. Antheneum, 1986.

Leckie, William H. *The Buffalo Soldiers: A Narrative of the Negro Cavalry in the West.* Norman: University of Oklahoma Press, 1985.

Logan, Rayford. W. and Michael R. Winston., eds. *Dictionary of American Negro Biography.* New York. W.W. Norton & Company, 1982.

Rust, Edna and Art. *Art Rust's Illustrated History of the Black Athlete.* New York: Doubleday & Company, 1985.

Williams, Juan. *Eyes on the Prize: America's Civil Rights Years 1954-1965.* New York: Viking, 1987.

Witherspoon, William Roger. *Martin Luther King, Jr., . . . To the Mountain Top.* New York: Doubleday & Company, 1985.

Index

Page numbers in boldface type indicate illustrations.

Picture Acknowledgments

American College of Surgeons—106
American Red Cross—161
AP/Wide World Photos, Inc.—Back cover (top right), front cover (Thurgood Marshall), 82, 104, 120, 131, 132, 135, 153, 155, 164, 166, 167, 169, 171, 173, 180, 188, 189, 191, 193, 194, 199, 202, 204, 214, 225
The Bettmann Archive—97, 184, 197
The Chicago *Defender*—127
Chicago Historical Society—12
Cincinnati Art Museum—53
The Daily Chronicle, Centralia, Washington—71
Denver Public Library, Western History Department—46
DePauw University—168
© Antonio Dickey—216
Frick Art Reference Library—23
H. Armstrong Roberts—7, 152, 195, 219
Historical Pictures Service, Chicago—Front cover (Martin L. King, Jr.), 14, 36, 45, 55, 56, 57, 67, 85, 91, 94, 95, 96, 101, 110, 112, 115, 126, 140, 146, 148, 157, 183
The Historical Society of Pennsylvania—22
Johnson Publishing Company—Front cover (Rosa Parks), 181
Frank Leslies Illustrated Newspaper—105
The Library Company of Philadelphia—28
Library of Congress—Front cover (Matthew Henson, Nat Love), 15, 18, 19, 27, 73, 87, 89, 118
Maryland Historical Society—16
Massachusetts Historical Society—26, 144, 145
Moorland-Spingarn Research Center, Howard University—Front cover (Ida B. Wells), 41, 61, 75, 99, 113, 121, 137, 150, 178
National Archives—162
NASA—Front cover (Guion Bluford), 212
National Park Service—Front cover (Harriet Tubman, Sojourner Truth), 63, 65
National Portrait Gallery, Smithsonian Institution, Washington, D.C.—43, 59, 123, 139, 141, 150, 159
Nebraska State Historical Society, Solomon D. Butcher Collection—90
The New York Public Library—Front cover (Mary Church Terrell), 116, 176
North Wind Picture Archives—Back cover (top left, center, bottom), 9, 21, 47, 49, 64, 70, 84, 240
Photri—77, 79
Sophia Smith Collection—Front cover (Frederick Douglass), 62, 69
UPI—201
U. S. Air Force Photo—175
USDA Photo—102
The Valentine Museum—24
The Walker Collection of A'Lelia Bundels—108
Courtesy The Carter Woodson Library—107
Yale University Art Gallery—20
Steven Dobson—8, 30, 33, 50, 54, 129, 133
George Nock—32, 35, 38, 48, 93

Gather out of star-dust
Earth-dust
Cloud-dust
Storm-dust,
And splinters of hail,
One handful of dream-dust
Not for sale.[16]

About the Author

Susan Altman is the author of the play, *Out of The Whirlwind*, and the producer of the Emmy Award-winning television programs "It's Academic," "It's Elementary," and "Pick Up the Beat." She lives in Washington, D.C.

About the Artists

Steven Gaston Dobson, a professional artist for over forty years, lives in Englewood, Florida. Known for his portraits and landscapes, Mr. Dobson has done murals and illustrations for children's books for several major publishing companies.

George Nock, a former running back with the New York Jets and the Washington Redskins, is a professional artist and sculptor living in Reston, Virginia. In addition to his interest in black themes, Mr. Nock is known for his detailed depictions of mythical figures and wildlife.

DUE DATE

DEC. 8 1992			
FEB 25 1993			
OCT. 06 1993			
NOV 1 0 2000			
MAY 1 7 1995			
APR 2 7 '00			
SEP , 6 '00			
APR 2 9 '00			
APR 1 4 2009			
		Printed in USA	